Mrs Bryson

Child Life in Chinese Homes

Mrs Bryson

Child Life in Chinese Homes

ISBN/EAN: 9783337004309

Printed in Europe, USA, Canada, Australia, Japan

Cover: Foto ©Andreas Hilbeck / pixelio.de

More available books at **www.hansebooks.com**

THE FOREIGNER IN FAR CATHAY.

[See Page 157.]

CHILD LIFE

IN

CHINESE HOMES.

BY

MRS. BRYSON,

OF THE LONDON MISSION, WUCHANG, CHINA.

With many Illustrations.

THE RELIGIOUS TRACT SOCIETY,

56, PATERNOSTER ROW; 65, ST. PAUL'S CHURCHYARD; AND 164, PICCADILLY.

1885.

TO THE DEAR MEMORY OF

Little Lillie,

BORN AT WUCHANG, ON THE YANG-TSE-KIANG; DIED AT CHEFOO, ON THE YELLOW SEA,

HER MOTHER DEDICATES THIS BOOK.

———

For dear e'en as my native shores
The land that owns her grave.

PREFACE.

—◦◦◦——

MORE than nine years ago I set sail for far-off China. Since then the city of Wuchang-fu, six hundred miles up the great Yang-tse-kiang, has been my home.

When I arrived there, how extraordinary the little pig-tailed boys and small-footed girls looked to me, and how much I wished to be able to understand them when they were chattering away to each other in words which sounded so strange to me!

After a while I learned to speak to them in their own language. They would follow me in large numbers along the narrow streets, and gather round me wonderingly as I sat down on the green slopes of their city wall. By-and-by some of them came to our schools, and became very well known to me.

Many Chinese children have paid me constant visits at the Mission House, the sick coming for medicines, the poor and those who were in trouble for relief and comfort. Not a few who were well and strong came also with their relatives to make friendly calls, and look at the strange things that were to be found in a "foreigner's" house

I have sojourned with Chinese children in their own little cottages among the mountains, and travelled with the boatmen's families across some of the great Chinese lakes, and down the broad river.

Some of them I have visited in their ancient homes, surrounded by lofty whitewashed walls, looking very gloomy outside, and very comfortless within, notwithstanding much grandeur of carved wood and painting.

The acquaintance of other children has been made as they crouched, half starved with cold and hunger, within the frail mat shed which they called home. Many a talk I have had with their mothers about our children; and the better I knew them the more earnestly I longed to do them good and make them happy. And now I want you to become acquainted with these Chinese children too.

You cannot all take the long journey to China, so I will tell you something of what I have seen, and write out for you the stories of a few of my young Chinese friends. When you have read the book, I trust that, knowing much more about China's children, you will wish to do more than you have ever done before to make them as happy as you are.

Should this be so, I shall feel very thankful and glad that I have told you a little of what I have seen and heard in the great land of China.

MARY ISABELLA BRYSON.

CONTENTS.

—⋅⋅—

PART I.

CHAP.		PAGE
I.	THE CHINESE BABY	11
II.	HIS HOME AND FRIENDS .	20
III.	THE SIGHTS HE SEES .	30
IV.	CHINESE BOYS AT SCHOOL	40
V.	CHINESE BOYS AT PLAY .	52
VI.	CHINESE GIRLS AT HOME	63
VII.	TWO BOY-EMPERORS OF CHINA	83
VIII.	CHINESE FESTIVALS AND HOLIDAYS .	89
IX.	CHINESE IDOLATRY AND SUPERSTITIONS .	. 101
X.	TEACHING CHINESE CHILDREN	. 117

PART II.

I.	YAU-TING ; OR, FIRST-FRUITS GATHERED .	. 129
II.	SHIN-KU ; OR, THE NEW DAUGHTER .	138

CONTENTS.

CHAP.   PAGE

III. CHIH-SHWIN; OR, THE MANDARIN'S LITTLE PAGE . . 148

IV. BRIGHT HOPES CLOUDED; OR, THE STORY OF A CHINESE
     SCHOOL-GIRL .   . 154

V. CHWIN-E; OR, THE FLOWER THAT FADED .   . 163

VI. YANG KIEN-TANG; OR, THE BOY WHO BECAME A DOCTOR 168

VII. KAI-KWEI; OR, THE YOUNG SOLDIER .   . 175

VIII. TA-KU AND ER-KU; OR, THE TEACHER'S DAUGHTERS . . 181

IX. HOW SWEI-KU WAS CURED OF RUNNING AWAY .   . 187

X. REFUSING TO BOW DOWN IN THE HOUSE OF RIMMON; OR,
    THE STORY OF CHANG-FU .   . . 190

XI. CHIANG-SWEI; OR, THE PREACHER'S SON .   195

XII. THE MANDARIN'S THREE DAUGHTERS   200

XIII. CONCLUSION   . 205

LIST OF ILLUSTRATIONS.

	PAGE
THE FOREIGNER IN FAR CATHAY	*Frontispiece*
A BABY TOWER .	16
THE BABY'S MOTHER .	21
THE BABY'S FATHER .	23
THE BABY'S HOME .	27
CHINESE CITY WALLS	31
A STREET BARBER .	35
FISHING ON THE YANG-TSE-KIANG	39
A BOYS' SCHOOL. .	41
THE PUNCH AND JUDY SHOW .	55
THE CRICKET FIGHT	57
ITINERANT TOYMAN . .	59
ITINERANT SELLER OF SWEETMEATS .	60
A CHINESE LANTERN AND BEARER	62
GOLDEN LILIES—BARE AND SHOD	70
THE BRIDAL CHAIR	79
PRINCE KUNG .	85
A STREET BEGGAR .	92
NEW YEAR'S MODE OF SALUTATION .	100

	PAGE
BUDDHIST PRIESTS . .	. 104
THE YELLOW STORK TOWER	. 106
WUCHANG .	. 107
ORPHAN ISLAND, POYANG LAKE	. 110
SERVICE FOR THE BENEFIT OF THE DEAD .	. 115
BOATS ON THE YANG-TSE RIVER	. 120
ARRIVAL OF A FOREIGNER	. 122
A VILLAGE AUDIENCE	144
ENTRANCE TO A YAMEN . .	. 151
CHINESE COURTYARD AND GARDEN	. 165
CHINESE CHESS PLAYERS	. 167
HANKOW, FROM THE HANYANG HILL	. 169
THE VICEROY LI HUNG-CHANG	. 171
THE CHINESE WORD FOR " FAITH "	. 173
CHINESE SOLDIERS	. 177
BOAT-TOWING IN CHINA	. 189
A CHINESE COURTYARD	. 201

PART I.

CHAPTER I.

THE CHINESE BABY.

PIGTAIL and almond-shaped eyes were the characteristic features of John Chinaman, or rather of the picture which fancy painted of him in my childhood's days.

My ideas upon the subject were gleaned from close study of the tea-chests, adorned with strange-looking figures in impossible attitudes, and from kindred works of art, painted on delicate chinaware.

I used to dream over the willow-pattern plate, with its wonderful picture-story. The bridge over which the three Celestials were running, the extraordinary foliage of the trees, the queer little boat with its one sailor, and the two doves which, hovering in mid-air, surveyed the scene,—all were objects of the keenest interest to me. It is a long time now since the days of which I am writing, yet the far-off "Middle Kingdom" and its strange inhabitants have only grown in attractiveness to me.

For many years past, my home has been within its boundaries; and to-day it seems almost as much "my ain countree," as the shores of dear old England.

Remembering, therefore, my youthful interest in that distant and wonderful land, I will ask you to walk with me through Chinese streets, to enter the strange homes so different from your own, to listen to the accents of the ancient language spoken by the people, and to make the acquaintance of some of the boys and girls whose lot has been cast there.

It is a long journey of more than ten thousand miles which I am asking you to take, before we shall reach the shores of that vast empire which is larger even than the continent of Europe, and is inhabited by more than a quarter of the human family.

In so large a country we have naturally every variety of climate. We have also lofty mountains whose peaks are always capped with snow, and mighty rivers, one of which, the grand Yang-tse-kiang, is the longest in all Asia. In the interior there are immense plains and splendid water communication. The Grand Canal, originally more than six hundred miles in length, unites the Yang-tse with the Yellow River, connecting Peking in the north with Hangchow in the centre.

Far away to the north rises the Great Wall of China, more than twelve hundred miles in length. It was built by one of the Chinese Emperors to keep out the Tartars; but it failed to accomplish the end for which it was built, since at the present time the Emperor of China is a Tartar.

Not only is China so extensive and grand a country, but it is the most ancient empire now in existence. In the far-off ages of the past, when Moses led the children of Israel out of Egypt, the Chinese were a strong nation, with laws and a literature of their own. Some ten years after the child Samuel heard the voice of God speaking to him in the still midnight hours, a Chinese Emperor named Wun Wang was writing a book, which is one of the standards of education in China to-day, and is committed to memory by all the advanced students in the empire. And when our own predecessors were only painted savages, wandering about the forests of Britain, the Chinese were enjoying a high degree of prosperity and civilization.

I will not, however, in the meantime, stay to write more of the country which they inhabit, but at once introduce to you some of the children of the land; for when you become acquainted with the training and manner of life of the young people of a country, you gain a pretty good idea of the kind of men and women they will become by-and-by.

Let us commence with the very beginning of life, and, going into one of these Chinese houses, have a peep at the baby, lying in his bamboo cradle, with its heavy framework and rockers, while his bright black eyes peer up at you curiously out of his small sallow face.

If it is summer-time, baby is not troubled with much clothing, a single airy garment being considered quite sufficient. During the cold days of winter, there being no fires lighted for warming Chinese houses, baby is muffled in so many tiny wadded garments that he looks like the queerest little ball imaginable. His clothes are not white, like an English child's, but of some bright colour, usually scarlet. Round his fat little wrists you will notice a red cord has been tied. This is considered by his parents a very important matter, and serious consequences are dreaded if it should be neglected. When a child is disobedient and difficult to manage, a common remark is, "Surely his parents forgot to bind his wrists," for this mysterious operation is practised with the idea of making the little fellow docile and obedient in future life. Round the baby's neck you will see another piece of red cord has been tied, and suspended from it are quite a number of small objects which are supposed to act as charms, preserving the little one from the attacks of evil spirits, and guarding him against numerous childish complaints. Here are a number of small copper coins with a hole through the centre. They are the only currency of China. After being nicely rubbed up, they are hung round baby's neck, and are supposed to insure his freedom from attacks of colic and other ailments of infancy. Some of the charms are in the form of fabulous animals; occasionally they are made of silver. But whatever the shape or material, they are a great source of satisfaction to the baby, who bites and jingles them with all the delight of an English child playing with its coral and bells. On the day that baby is a fortnight old special thanksgiving is made, and offerings are laid before the family shrine of the goddess called "Mother."

But the most important event in the early days of a Chinese baby is the occasion on which his first month of life is celebrated. If baby is a boy, and particularly a first-born son, all the relatives and connections from far and near are invited to come to a grand feast in honour of the happy day. No one is expected to arrive empty-handed; and baby's riches in the way of silver rings, charms, and lucky cash, not to mention painted ducks'-eggs, and piles of sweetmeats and cakes, have accumulated considerably before the day is over. The great event of the day is the shaving of the child's head. Chinese nurses are amazed to find that English boys and girls, whose mothers neglect this important duty, can still boast of flowing locks when the years of childhood are past. The baby's head is shaved before the ancestral tablets, or the shrine of " Mother," and the barber who performs the delicate operation, though he makes no charge, finds it the most profitable part of his business, since a money present is willingly given.

The baby's grandmother has an important part to play on this occasion: she is the principal guest of the day, and if she belongs to the wealthier classes, the presents she sends are generally numerous and costly. The most important of these is a gay little cap, ornamented with embroidery, and eighteen gold, silver, or copper figures of the disciples of Buddha, which are believed to attract all good influences towards their little wearer.

On the same day, baby receives his " Milk " or pet name : but this does not of course serve him all his life through, for when he is old enough to go to school, the master selects a name for him ; and later on, when he is married, or if he is fortunate enough to succeed in the competitive examinations, he will probably receive yet a third name.

These Milk names are sometimes very extraordinary to English ears ; for the parents are afraid to give their children the fine high-sounding names their love suggests, lest the evil spirits, of whom they stand in constant fear, should come to understand how precious they are, and cause some calamity to overtake them.

And so you constantly meet with children answering to the names of Little Stupid, Vagabond, Flea, Dirt, or Spring Dog,—the idea being that when the spirits hear the little ones called by such uncomplimentary names, they will imagine that the parents care very little for them, and will not take the trouble to molest them.

This foreboding that disaster may befall a child, particularly an only son, is the reason why many little boys wear the dress of a Buddhist priest, and have their heads kept shaved till they are eight or nine years of age. By that time, if they are strong and well, they are dressed like other boys; the period of anxiety is supposed to have passed, and the parents imagine they have successfully deceived the spirits, by the ruse of making it appear they cared so little for their son that they were willing to make him a Buddhist priest.

And now, at the very beginning of the baby's life, you will find how widely the customs of China differ from those of our own land. In England, whether the baby is a boy or a girl, it is welcomed and loved by its parents; and in a family the little girls are considered as precious as their brothers. But in China it is quite different.

When the news of a baby's birth is sent to the relatives and friends, the sex of the child is the most important part of the announcement. If it is a boy, rejoicings are general, and all the friends call upon the family with presents and congratulations. But if the baby is a girl, the parents are considered to be more in need of sympathy than congratulation, and the kindest remark any soft-hearted visitor can possibly be expected to make is, "Ah, well, even girls are of some use!"

Not unfrequently when a little girl is born, its parents will drown it rather than have the trouble of bringing it up. Some women have destroyed as many as five or six little girls in this way. To save the babies from being put to death, kindhearted Chinamen have established Foundling Hospitals in many Chinese cities. The tiny baby-girls are taken in there when cast off by their fathers and mothers, and are given out in great numbers to country-women to nurse. It is a strange sight, once a month, to see these little foundlings being brought in from their country homes with their foster-mothers, and taken to the Foundling Hospital for inspection. Some come in small round baskets slung

A BABY TOWER.

from the end of a long pole, carried on a man's shoulders. If the babies are plump and well, the nurses receive their pay, but if they look thin or ailing, a considerable reduction is made in their wages. Many other Foundling Hospitals have been established by the Roman Catholics; and it is not unusual for the wife of a Protestant missionary to hear the low wail of a new-born baby-girl, which has been left upon the doorstep of the Mission House by parents who, though not willing to take the baby's life, were very anxious to get rid of it. Sometimes a man is employed to go round with a number of children, and try to dispose of them for money. One of our missionary friends in the Fuh-kien province was offered the chance of purchasing three little wailing babies, hungry and cold, after being carried with several others round for sale through a long day. If she would take the lot, the baby merchant said she should have them cheap.

If a Chinese baby dies, no loving hands prepare it for its grave. A piece of coarse matting is tied around the tiny body, and it is carried to a little tower erected outside most cities, with little openings like windows, but without doors. All that is left of baby is thrown in through one of these openings, and falls into the pit below the tower. If the little one is a girl, the parents are not always particular to ascertain if it is quite dead or not. The very fact of a baby's death convinces the parents that the little one was no precious gift to be treasured, but possessed by some evil spirit, and only the source of anxiety and misfortune from the first, and the sooner they forget all about it the better.

The baby-girl's head is shaved, but with few of the rejoicings that attend the same event in her brother's life; and she very frequently receives some such name as Chien-ti, "Lead along a brother;" Lai-ti, "Come younger brother"—with the idea of expressing the hope that she may soon be succeeded by a baby-boy. Sometimes, if she is the second or third child in a family, she is called simply, Daughter number one, or two, as the case may be. Occasionally some more poetical designation is chosen, such as Pearl, Fragrance, or Peace; or the name of a flower is selected, as Narcissus, Lily, or Rose.

After the shaving festival, baby is carried out to pay its first visit to its grandmother. On this occasion she presents the child with a number of small gifts, each of which has some good signification. Several kinds of vegetables which attain to maturity very rapidly are offered, as expressing the old lady's desire that baby may likewise quickly grow strong and sturdy; and rice husks, which signify that it is her wish that her small grandson should grow up a proficient scholar and a famous man. When the baby reaches the age of four months he is taught to sit in a chair, and so relieve his mother or attendant of the care of nursing him. Soft sugar-candy is placed on the little chair, and it is thought that henceforth baby will be very fond of sitting in it.

When the child goes out of doors he is frequently strapped upon the back of his attendant; the women of the poorer classes, while carrying their children in that position, manage to attend to most of their domestic duties.

A solemn, patient little being is the Chinese baby in general, putting up with indignities which an English child would violently resent. But he can laugh with the merriest when his mother holds him up to her face, not to kiss, but to smell the soft brown cheek. He likes to hear the strangely unmusical voice, in which she drones out the high notes of the " Mo li wha," or some other popular tune, and claps his small hands together gleefully to the nursery rhyme of :—

> One, strike the hand ;
> Two, let us play ;
> Three, draw the bow.

The day that is kept with greater rejoicings than any other in the baby's life is the anniversary of his birth. A great feast is spread, to which even the most distant relatives are invited, and every dainty known to the cuisine of China decks the festal board.

Presents, as usual, come pouring in on all sides ; but the most suitable offering is supposed to be a pair of embroidered shoes, since baby will soon be thinking of walking alone. Very gay indeed are the slippers, which have been worked by the skilful fingers of all the female relatives. Some are embroidered with the head of a cat, thereby expressing a hope that baby may become as sure-footed as pussy has the character of being. Some are decorated with the head of a frog, others have pretty floral designs, and yet another will bear the mystic symbol whose signification is, " May all you wish be yours."

After the feast, a very important ceremony is performed. The little scarlet-coated hero of the day is placed in the middle of a table which usually stands just in front of the ancestral tablets. Around the little man are ranged a great variety of articles, such as a mandarin's button and necklace, books, inkslab and pencil, a string of cash, artificial flowers, and other things significant of various professions and trades. The question of the day is, which object will attract the baby's attention, and, being grasped by his tiny hand, indicate his future career in life. The baby's grandmother is usually exceedingly careful to have the articles of best omen nearest to the child's hand. But if the baby chance to do his duty and grasp the glittering button and beads, the excitement is intense, and congratulatory phrases are heard on every side.

Very numerous are the thanksgivings and propitiatory services performed at some idol-temple, or before the family shrine, during the first two years of the baby's life. All of them are attended with burning of incense and paper money, letting off of crackers to frighten away evil spirits, and din of gongs and cymbals. But I will not stay to describe these further. We have seen the baby safely through the first year of his life, and will go on to speak of his friends and home, of the sights he sees around him, and the strange sounds his little lips soon learn to form.

CHAPTER II.

WHEN first the bright black eyes of the Chinese baby begin to gaze with some intelligence upon the strange new world in which it has come to live, the sights it sees are, for the most part, very different from those which attract the notice of an English child.

The first object of deepest interest with our baby Chinaman, as with his English brother, is always the face of his mother. And how unlike she is to an English mother! She has dark eyes, like the baby's, and raven locks, which are drawn tightly back from her face, and used to cover a queer framework, looking like butterflies' wings, or some other fantastic shape. Her forehead appears very broad, since, just before her wedding-day, all the short hairs over her brow were drawn out to give it this wide, open appearance.

Several of her finger nails are very long, for that is a sign that she is a lady, and has little work to do with her hands. To keep these nails from breaking, she wears over them little shields of gold or silver. But look at her feet! Could any one ever imagine that they were the feet of a grown-up woman? They have been bound and compressed with strong cotton bandages from her childhood, and now she can wear tiny slippers only three inches long, made of bright-coloured satin, and very beautifully embroidered. Every one admires her very much, and says that when she moves it is as the "waving of the willow trees," and they call her poor distorted feet "golden lilies." As we look at her our wonder is how she can manage to walk at all without coming to grief.

Her dress also looks strange to European eyes. She wears a loose tunic of some bright-flowered silk, trimmed with braid which is woven with silk and gold thread. Her sleeves are more than a yard round, and adorned with strips of beautiful embroidery. She wears loose trousers underneath the tunic, and when in full dress a kilted skirt, which is also richly trimmed. She can boast of a large stock of jewellery, and she wears many pins of elaborate workmanship in her dark locks. Her ears are quite weighed down by her large heavy earrings, and she has several rings upon her fingers, and massive bracelets on her arms.

When relatives and friends are invited to dine at their house,

THE BABY'S MOTHER.

the baby's mother never sits down to a meal with them. She remains always in her own apartment; but sometimes, when there is a merry company in the guest hall, you may hear a rustling and a sound of hushed laughter, and so be made aware of the fact that the lady of the house and her attendants are having a sly peep at what is going on ; or it is easy to make small holes in the paper screens, or to peer from behind a curtain which shields the door.

The baby's mother is quite unable to read or write, and very wearily the days pass with her. It takes a long time for her attendant to dress her hair, and fix it in its place with long pins and a sort of glue. Then she adorns it with bright-coloured, sweet-scented flowers. Her face also has to be powdered, and a touch of rouge put on here and there.

By-and-by she will spend a little time at her embroidery frame, or play with baby till she gets tired even of that amusement. Afterwards she takes a turn at smoking or card-playing, and so the weary hours of the day slip by.

It is quite a relief when every few days she has a call from one of the ancient dames who make their living by flower-selling, fortune-telling, or vending numerous small wares. Others come also who are employed as marriage makers, and go from one family to another trying to earn a living by arranging matches between babies or little children. But, whatever their profession, they are always very welcome visitors, since, with their lively gossip, and news of the families of their various clients, they bring a fresh breeze from the outer world into the close, stifling atmosphere of the "inner apartments."

As I have said, the baby's mother rarely goes outside the door of her own house ; but, on one or two occasions during the year, she is allowed to venture out in a sedan chair, with curtains closely drawn, carried on the shoulders of several coolies.

Once, in the early spring-time, she pays a visit to the family graves. She journeys outside the city walls, beyond the great plain dotted with countless numbers of mounds, marked by no tree or flower, but interspersed here and there by heavy coffins bound round by coarse strips of matting. Just on the borders of this city of the dead, which her sad heathen faith brightens with no ray of

THE BABY'S FATHER.

hope and peace, are the graves of the baby's forefathers for many generations. No better spot could possibly have been chosen, according to the geomancers who have been consulted about the matter, for behind it rises a green hill, sheltering the bones of the dead from chill northern blasts, while the warm southern sun shines in front upon the strangely-shaped granite slabs. With her own hands she has prepared the dishes of various kinds of food for an offering to the dead, but she stands aside while the male portion of the family entreat the spirits to come and partake of the feast provided for them, worshipping them meanwhile in reverential attitudes with smoke of burning incense and paper money.

At other times, especially if her baby is ill, she pays a visit to some noted temple, and there vows before the shrine of the Goddess of Mercy, or the idol called " Mother," that if they will but protect her darling and restore him to health again, costly offerings shall be laid at their feet.

As for the baby's father, his hair also is shaved off his forehead, and he wears the rest of it twisted into a heavy plait, which hangs down his back. To make it look long and thick, the barber often adds some false hair to it, or some threads of black silk. He wears a long robe of coloured silk, and in winter a sleeveless wadded vest of satin. In very cold weather he dresses in fur-lined robes. On ordinary occasions his head is covered with a skullcap of black silk, except when the weather is warm, and then he wears no covering at all. His official hat is made of felt, turned up all round, and trimmed with dark fur. The button or glass ball which tells the rank to which he has attained is fastened on the top of it. These balls are of various colours, and indicate the exact rank of the wearer. The highest is of red coral ; others are light red, light blue, dark blue, mother-of-pearl, and the lowest of all is a gilt ball. His shoes are made of satin, and have thick white soles, instead of being bright with blacking.

Baby's father is probably a scholar, and yet if you began to question him you would be inclined to consider him rather ignorant. He can quote whole chapters of the Chinese classics, and tell you in a moment the exact place in which any passage occurs, at the same time giving you some interpretation of it. But if you put him through the simplest examination in geography, you would find that the only clear idea he had upon the subject was that China was the largest and most important empire under the sun, and that whatever other small countries there might be beside were all tributary to it, and inhabited by "outer barbarians." He is always congratulating himself upon being born in the grand Celestial Empire, and feels convinced that the people of all other nations must be envious of his birthright.

As for the religion of the baby's father, he has little faith in the worship of idols, but he never fails to burn paper-money and incense before the carved wooden tablets in which he believes the spirits of his ancestors are dwelling. Not only does he love his baby-boy with the strong affection of a father, but all his hopes for future happiness are resting on that little life.

If so terrible a misfortune as his baby-son's death should overtake him, he believes when his turn comes to enter the unseen world his untended spirit will wander about those mysterious regions hungry and naked, homeless and miserable; for only a living son, by constant acts of devotion before the ancestral tablet and at the family graves, can supply the wants of a father in the spirit-land.

No wonder, then, that when the baby-boy was ailing, the proud father condescended to go begging from door to door in the city, asking each family, to the number of one hundred, for a single cash, a coin of which it takes twenty to make a penny. His idea was that the prayers and good wishes of each of these families would follow their money, and thus secure the health and prosperity of his child; and he purchased with the coins he collected a "hundred families lock," which is always worn round his little son's neck. No wonder, also, that when the baby was seriously ill, he walked through the city streets, carrying the child's small garments at the end of a bamboo pole, and crying out at intervals, "Return, return," for he believed that some evil spirit had tempted the little one's soul away and caused its sickness. How true it is that, in China, the life and future happiness of the parents are all bound up in the life of their child !

How different is the house in which the baby lives from the homes we love in dear old England ! It is of one story only, and the rooms are ranged one behind each other, with an open court between, called a t'ien ching, or " heavenly well," which is very prettily decorated. In the centre you will see some curious rockwork, and over or among it strange-looking dwarf plants and shrubs are growing. Here is a fir tree no taller than a geranium, stunted and bound with fine wire, till it looks the queerest little dwarf imaginable. Close by the rockwork you will see little tanks in which gold and silver fish are kept, and others in which the broad leaves of the lotus, with its delicate pink flowers, are growing. All around the court are pretty earthenware stands upon which pots of flowers are placed. Here are beautiful dwarf orange trees, the golden fruit gleaming out from among the dark, glossy leaves and fragrant buds. There are also stately oleanders and brilliant pomegranate buds, and many more besides. In some quiet corner, wisteria, jessamine and climbing Chinese roses grow luxuriantly; and in the autumn, the sweet scent of the " Kwei-wha," or flower of the fragrant olive, is borne on every breeze.

We have stopped in our description of the house to talk about the garden, which would be quite out of place if it were in England; but in China, as I said before, it is different, for houses there are often built round the garden, instead of the garden going round the house.

Passing on into the principal room of the mansion, which is called the "guest hall," we find it furnished with a large oblong daïs or couch, with a low stand in the centre. It is placed near to the wall of the apartment, just opposite the door. Large illuminated scrolls are suspended on the wall in pairs, having selected passages from the Chinese classics written upon them. If there is no hall set apart for the ancestral tablets, they are usually found in this room. On either side we see elaborately carved chairs, placed in pairs opposite

THE BABY'S HOME.

to each other, with a tea-stand between each. All Chinese rooms are furnished in exactly the same fashion, and when a visitor enters the house he knows exactly in what light you regard him by the worth of the seat you press him to take. The seat of honour is on the left hand of the host.

There is no fire-place in the apartment, for the Chinese have no stoves for heating rooms, though in the northern parts of the empire a broad hollow bench of brick is erected and heated by flues. Being without glass windows, even on a bright day the room is dull; but when the handsome lanterns which are suspended from the ceiling are lighted up, it has a pretty effect. A side door, often screened by a curtain, leads into the apartments of the women, which are always situated at the back of the house. Chinese doors and windows rarely fit very closely, and the only arrangement the people have for keeping themselves warm is to heap on jacket after jacket, and vest after vest, till they seem almost smothered with clothing. The poor people pad their jackets with cotton wool, and those who can afford it wear fur-lined garments. They warm their hands and feet with small hand and foot stoves, which look like little brass baskets with grated covers, filled with charcoal embers. The "sou-lou," or hand stove, is very small and light, and is frequently pushed up the large Chinese sleeves.

Going into the sleeping rooms, we find bedsteads not unlike our own. There are, however, no blankets or sheets, and a large wadded coverlet, gay with bright chintz, forms both mattress and covering. We see no soft feather pillows, but in summer-time only a hard frame of bamboo, which keeps the head cool. In winter a different pillow is used, embroidered at the ends and covered with cloth : this also is very stiff and hard.

When we come to the commissariat of China, we shall find that even the food is very different from our own. When a Chinaman meets you he does not ask after your health, but his polite greeting is, "Have you taken your rice?"—and rice is the universal "staff of life" in South and Central China.

In the baby's home, knives and forks are never seen upon the table, but only two sticks, about a foot long, made either of ivory or varnished wood. Chop-sticks is the name given to these useful little articles by foreigners, but the Chinese themselves call them kwai-tsz, or "quick lads."

At meal-time each person has his own special basin of rice, which he holds up very near to his mouth; then taking the chop-sticks in his right hand, he manages to empty his basin and be ready for another in a very short space of time. Vegetables, fish, and meat are also cooked and placed in separate basins in the centre of the table, and when any one wishes for a relish to his rice, he dips his chop-sticks into the common dish and secures a morsel. The Chinese think our English fashion of serving large joints of meat on the table quite unworthy of a civilized nation. They say they leave the work of carving and preparing the food to their servants, but we keep our guests waiting while we do it ourselves at table.

A Chinese feast frequently lasts for many hours. The table is usually bare, no cloth of any kind being spread upon it. Dessert, consisting generally of dried fruits, nuts, etc., is placed first upon the festive board. One plate is considered sufficient for each guest, however large the number of courses may be, and sometimes there are as many as twenty-five different dishes. Birds'-nest soup, sea-slugs, or *bêche de mer*, sharks' fins, and ducks' tongues are some of the peculiar dishes which appear at a Chinese feast. Nearly everything is stewed, and flavoured with garlic or oil, which makes these dainties not very agreeable to a European palate. Frequently, when foreign guests have been invited, the cook is ordered to flavour the dishes sparingly, in order to suit the strange Western taste. Wine is served hot in China, and poured from zinc or silver kettles into the daintiest of small porcelain wine-cups. Tea is always kept in the house ready for drinking, and when a visitor calls, a servant immediately brings in a cup of the national beverage, which is served without sugar or milk.

CHAPTER III.

WHEN for the first time a Chinese child goes out of doors, and is carried in the arms, or sits with his legs round the neck of his attendant, it is a very busy world he enters, and a strange one also to Western eyes. As he passes along the streets in most parts of China, he finds even the widest and busiest in the city are narrower than our English lanes ; they have no side walks, and are paved with irregular stone slabs, for it is considered unlucky to have them laid down evenly. There are no open spaces or squares in the midst of a Chinese city, but all the houses are packed together in the smallest possible space. Being built largely of wood, the frequent fires constantly destroy whole streets at a time. But the householders begin to build again among the smoking ashes, setting up stalls close by the ruins, and attempting to carry on their business as best they can under the circumstances.

Most Chinese cities are surrounded by strong walls, with gates which are well defended ; frequently they are closed at sunset, and no exit or entrance is permitted till daylight. A small guard of soldiers is often posted at the gates for their defence. Chinese soldiers are strangely destitute of that air of briskness and general vigour which is so characteristic of our military men. Their uniform is usually of blue cotton, loose in shape, and occasionally they have a jacket or vest of scarlet. This garment is adorned with a white disc, bearing characters which describe the regiment to which they belong.

Turning back from the gate into the street, we shall find it damp with the drippings from the water-buckets which the coolies have been carrying from the river since early morning. A pretty vista of

CHINESE CITY WALLS.

bright colouring meets our eyes, formed by the signboards, which are not placed over the doors only, as in England, but hang down perpendicularly from the projecting eaves. Many of them are eight or ten feet long, and are nicely varnished and inscribed with some high-flown epithet, which has been chosen by the owner instead of his name. And so we meet with a furrier's shop bearing the title " Virtuous and Abundant," and a cloth store called " Celestial Advantage." An undertaker has chosen the title of " United and Prosperous," and a coal merchant calls his premises by the high-sounding name of " Heavenly Adornment." In summer-time the streets are shaded with matting, to protect the passers-by from the fierce rays of the sun.

No carts or carriages are seen in Chinese streets, and only an occasional horseman, riding in some mandarin's procession. Sedan chairs are in constant use, varying in size and appearance from the official's roomy and elaborately decked conveyance to the fragile bamboo erections which are found at corners of the thoroughfares waiting to be hired, as hansoms stand on the streets of English cities. It seems wonderful that room can be found for the chairs readily to pass and repass in a Chinese street, but the coolies press on through the thronging crowds, shouting at the top of their voices, " Look out for your backs ! Look out for your backs ! "

Here are some coolies carrying baskets of rice to the public granaries, while others are heavily laden with buckets, full of water from the river or lake. Step by step as they plod along they drone out their monotonous carrying song, " Hay ho ! High ho ! "

Here is a man with his baskets filled with the glossy brown pods which are used as soap by the natives. Yonder comes a lantern-seller, with fifty or more skeletons of lanterns at each end of his long pole ; it is wonderful to see the dexterity with which he avoids mishaps, and manages with his cumbersome burden to make his way through the crowded streets. Now we are thrust to the side of the road by an immense water-buffalo, upon whose unwieldy form his keeper, in the shape of a small boy, is mounted. Immediately after we meet a pig in a large cylindrical bamboo basket, slung on a long pole and carried by two bearers. The Chinese consider it more expeditious to carry piggy to market than to attempt to drive him through their narrow streets. Close upon the heels of the pig and his bearers comes the procession of some high mandarin. The great man sits at ease in his richly decorated sedan-chair, preceded by a very shabby-looking retinue. He wears handsome robes of satin, and an expression of impassive superiority rests upon his solemn countenance. At the head of the great man's procession appear one or two couples of lictors, armed with whips and wearing tall conical-shaped felt hats. Behind them comes a string of small boys, frequently the Arabs of the streets; they carry large painted boards upon which the characters "Stand aside," and "Let there be respectful silence," appear. Last of all comes the characteristic umbrella or many-flounced scarlet canopy, which is held aloft above the great man's head whenever he alights from his sedan.

Notwithstanding the narrowness of Chinese streets, the space is still further restricted by the erection before the open shop fronts of numerous small stalls. Here is the establishment of a travelling tinker; by his side is the stand of a wandering physician. Opposite to them we see sitting at a small table the money-changer, with his strings of cash, his scales, and broken pieces of silver. By his side sits the spectacle-mender, the migratory barber, and the travelling cook.

Let us stop for a moment at this itinerant cookshop, and take a look at some of the viands which are pressed upon us. We are not likely to find the puppies, snails and kittens of which we have perhaps heard, but here are sausage balls flavoured with garlic, minced beef mixed with appetizing celery, delicate slices of fried fish, dumplings of fat pork flavoured with sugar, and griddle cakes fried a beautiful gold colour. No wonder that with such a display of delicacies these stalls are liberally patronised, and constantly surrounded by a group of men taking their meal in this expeditious fashion.

Passing by the barber, who drives a brisk trade, since most Chinamen have their heads shaved every few days, we will spend

D

a few minutes at the stall of the well-patronised fortune-teller. They profess to be able to predict the future in various ways, by dissection of the written character, by tortoises and by birds.

A young man approaches with an anxious look upon his countenance, and informs the diviner that he purposes leaving home for a season, and would like to know if his journey will be prosperous or not. "Going from home," says the fortune-teller, as he calls from his cage the wisest and most old-fashioned of birds, tempting him out with a grain of rice. Then he shuffles a pack of cards containing answers to imaginary questions, and birdie is directed to pick one out. He does so, and the fortune-teller reads the answer to the effect that "The journey will not be prosperous. You will lose money by it. Stay at home for a little while till a more favourable opportunity."

But what is this string of blind men following in single file, holding by each other's garments? They are the blind beggars going on their rounds. They go from shop to shop, each tradesman giving them a small sum, except in cases where the householders pay them an annual subscription, and are thus relieved of their calls altogether.

Here are some more beggars, for they are a numerous class in China. They sit on the bare earth, and sometimes have a heart-rending account of their difficulties written on the pavement before them or painted on a board. They seem to be in very distressing circumstances, and as they entreat the "honourable passer-by" to spare them a single cash they knock their foreheads violently against the hard stones of the footpath. Frequently we observe that they have exercised considerable forethought, since their heads are protected by a thick leather pad, upon which the force of their violent "ko-tows" or head knockings expends itself.

Here comes a beggar of another kind; it is a mendicant priest. He wears a loose yellow robe, his head is completely shaved, and no queue of braided hair hangs down his back. Around his waist is fastened a wooden drum, which he taps as he walks along. This curious instrument is used in the temples as an accompaniment to the prayers of the priests; the sound it emits when struck is

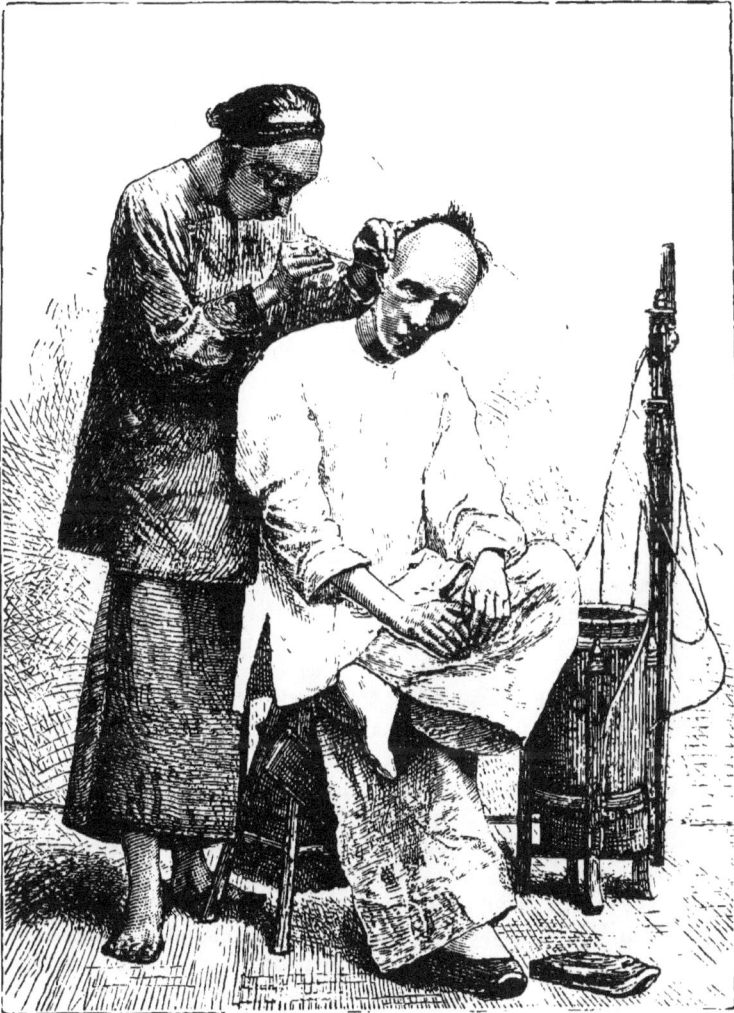

A STREET BARBER.

peculiarly dull and hollow. These mendicant priests are usually chosen from among the rest on account of their superior sanctity. They carry a small wallet strapped upon the back, to receive the contributions of the faithful, who are taught that he who helps a priest contributes to his own advancement in the future world.

Many of the shop fronts are gay with flowers, which are planted in elegant flower-pots brought from the far-famed potteries of Chin-teh-tsin, on the Poyang Lake. The Chinese are fond of flowers, and the florist drives a good trade. See him as he approaches with his shallow bamboo baskets, filled with fine plants which it has been his aim through careful cultivation to induce to bear blossoms of the largest size possible. In the early spring he has the fragrant flowers of the la-mei and the delicate pink blossoms of the almond. Later on there are brilliant azaleas, roses, pinks, and peonies, pomegranates and water-lilies, and with the cool breezes of early autumn come the gorgeous coxcombs of stately height with gigantic flowers. The delicate, many-tinted chrysanthemums are the pride of Chinese gardeners, with the beautiful blossoms of the passion-flower and the aster. Then the faint, sweet scent of the kwei-wha, or fragrant olive, is wafted on every breeze, and Nature's incense seems for a time almost to overpower the vile odours which rise from the crowded streets of every Chinese city.

Our friend the florist is usually paid a certain annual sum by wealthy householders, and engages in return to keep their courtyards and gardens gay with flowers the whole year round, finding even in the dull winter days " things of beauty," in the shape of the fragrant narcissus and the delicate camellia, to adorn these Chinese homes.

I have said there are no squares in most Chinese cities, the nearest approach to them being the open spaces sometimes seen in front of temples, or the courtyards of yamens, or magistrates' offices. The latter are frequently adorned with extraordinary stone figures of animals which the Chinese call lions. They are objects of awe to all Chinese children, who hear weird stories of how the lions are only stone lions in the day-time, but at night they come to life and wander through the streets of the city.

We have been wandering for some time through the busy thorough-fares of a Chinese town, and now let us enter one of the shops, and try to do a little business with the comfortable-looking tradesman who sits at his ease at the other side of the counter, and is probably very leisurely smoking his pipe. We will suppose that we have entered a store stocked with the far-famed earthenware of the Celestial Empire. Here are magnificent vases, five feet high, adorned with groups of figures painted in delicate colours ; close by are barrel-shaped stands for flower-pots gaily ornamented, and all kinds of household utensils. Here are wine pots, delicate teacups, and a large number of articles which have been produced to supply the demand from foreign countries, such as tea sets of English fashion, with handles to the cups, and saucers ; little teapots, which are rarely used by the natives; and fanciful ornaments of all shapes and sizes. The shopkeeper finds us the article for which we are seeking, and calmly asks us about twice the sum which we know it to be worth. We promptly reply that it is far too dear, and he slightly reduces the price. This sort of bargain-ing continues for a considerable time, and ends by our eventually paying him half the price he first asked us—to his intense satisfaction, since he has profited considerably by his dealings with the outer barbarian, who has doubtless given him a far larger sum for his wares than he would receive from one of his own countrymen. Before we leave—indeed in the midst of our bargaining—a cup of tea has been presented to us, and a pipe pressed upon our notice.

But what is the business of the man who is approaching us, carrying two large deep bamboo baskets, with a tiny flag attached to one of them bearing the legend, " Respect printed paper " ? As he proceeds, a door here and there opens, and a man-servant comes out with a waste basket, emptying its contents into the large basket carried by the collector of scraps. This man is employed by some Chinese benevolent society to go round and collect even the smallest pieces of printed paper, so that they may be carried to some temple courtyard and destroyed by fire in a furnace set apart for the purpose, for the kitchen stove would be considered too secular a place for performing such a sacred duty. This is one of the works of merit which the Chinese believe accumulate for them a sort of balance, to be set against the sins they have committed when they are judged by the king of the infernal regions at the end of life.

Probably few things have contributed so much to the idea that foreigners are uncivilized barbarians as our light regard for our own printed or written paper. They see us using it in all sorts of ignominious ways. We wrap up parcels in it, and frequently carelessly tread it underfoot, consequently the Chinese not unnaturally conclude that we can have nothing worthy of the name of a language or literature, or we should not treat the printed page in so disrespectful a manner.

Now we are passing a fine tea-shop, the great rendezvous of all Chinamen. There they sit in large numbers, discussing the topics of the day, while the national beverage is freely imbibed. Melon-seeds and pea-nuts are also provided at these establishments, and are taken with the tea. A Chinaman will pass the greater part of a day in one of these places of public resort, spending probably only a penny.

Before we leave these crowded streets, let us look at some of the names which they bear. Many of them are very high-sounding, and this is most frequently the case when the locality is low and of bad repute. First we have the street of Perpetual Comfort, and near by is the Lane of Filial Piety, and the Court of Eternal Harmony. Then there is the lane of the Chia Family, New Street, Horse-tail Lane, Thread and Needle Alley, and the street of Heavenly Treasures.

As we leave the city we pass through two heavy stone gateways; outside them the heads of criminals are frequently suspended in small bamboo cages—a ghastly sight which seems to be little heeded by the passers-by, although they are placed there to awaken terror in the hearts of evil-doers.

Beneath the gateways we shall see various notices and advertisements pasted up. Announcements of approaching religious festivals, or the ordination services of some Buddhist priests, are there. Advertisements to push the sale of kerosine oil, anti-opium pills, and other quack medicines, and notices of rewards offered for the discovery of persons who are missing from their homes.

So, with much that is totally different, we find many points of similarity between the customs and sights of this ancient empire and our own English towns, and most probably return from our wanderings with the reflection that human nature is pretty much the same the whole world over.

FISHING ON THE YANG-TSE-KIANG.

CHAPTER IV.

WHEN a Chinese boy reaches his sixth birthday, it is considered quite time he should be sent to school.

The occasion is looked upon as one of such importance that a fortune-teller is usually consulted, and on a lucky day, fixed upon by the wise man, the little Chinaman makes his first appearance at school. Let us follow him when, accompanied by his father, he makes his way to the school-house. He looks very fresh and tidy, his hair has been neatly shaved from his forehead, and the rest of it is plaited up into a long black queue, a pien-tsz he calls it, which hangs down behind. When any of his school-fellows want to torment him, they will no doubt tie his pigtail to the same appendage on another boy's head, which will be very uncomfortable for them both.

If it is summer-time, our young friend wears nothing upon his head, and is only clothed in a jacket or vest of loose cotton or grass-cloth, with small baggy trousers of the same material. But if the weather is cold, he will, no doubt, be wearing half a dozen vests and coats, one above another, and some of them will be padded with cotton-wool. The first thing that strikes you, as you look at him, is how very difficult he must find it to make any use of his arms. Upon his head he wears a small skullcap of black or blue silk, with a little scarlet twist at the top, and very likely a thick tassel of silken threads falling down behind. His shoes have very thick white soles, and very often the toes are embroidered by his proud mother with fanciful little designs of flowers or butterflies. Sometimes he wears in his girdle a little purse, which has also been embroidered by his

A BOYS' SCHOOL.

mother, but it will not hold many of the copper coins with a hole through the centre, which we call "cash." If he is ever rich enough to have saved any number of these coins, he strings them on a wisp of straw or piece of string, making a firm knot at each end to keep them safe.

If he does not possess a purse, he is at no loss for a receptacle for his boyish treasures, since his sleeves are so large and long that they form a capital hiding-place. In China, little books are not called pocket editions, but sleeve editions; a man does not pocket anything, as in England, but he "sleeves" it.

Having reached the school-house, our boy-friend enters, carrying in his hand some small present for the grave-looking elderly person who is to be his teacher, and his first act is to do reverence and burn incense before the tablet which has the name of the sage Confucius written upon it. The furniture of the room consists of a number of little desks or tables, with high stools behind them, which are frequently provided by the parents. Before the master stands a larger table, and upon it are lying not only books and papers, but the indispensable pipe. Upon each little desk you will see, not pens and ink such as we use in England, but inkstones, upon which the boys rub the cake of Indian, or rather Chinese ink, dipping it in a little water.

For his pen he has a brush, not unlike our large paint brushes of camel's hair. He holds it perpendicularly in his hand, pointing to the ceiling, as he traces on the thin soft paper the queer-looking characters on his copy slips.

English boys would doubtless consider Chinese lessons extremely dry and uninteresting, since several years have to be spent in learning to repeat the mere sounds and write the forms of the characters or picture-words, of the meaning of which they understand little more than a parrot.

There is no alphabet of the Chinese language, but two hundred and fourteen radicals or root words, which enter into the formation of all the other characters. The words are all of one syllable, and are written down one beneath the other in columns, instead of across the page, and the beginning of their books is the end of ours.

The language of China is so ancient that most people think it goes back to a time not long after the Deluge, and it is the oldest language now spoken in the world. The Chinese say that their written words or characters were originally hieroglyphics, or rough pictures of the objects of which they desired to speak.

To make my meaning clearer, I will write down a few of the pictures drawn by the ancient Chinese, and the names attached to them, and beneath these you will see the shapes of the characters as they are now written :—

Hieroglyph : ☉   ☽   大   ᨓ   馬

Present character : 日   月   子   山   馬
                    Sun   Moon Child Hill Horse

It was soon found quite impossible to express the requirements of a people in a language necessarily so limited as one made up of picture signs alone. Gradually the scholars began to use more complicated symbols, and frequently a picture word was used in combination with some other symbol to make the meaning plain :—

And so the sun 日 above the horizon, — signified morning, and is now written thus 旦

A tree is 木 ; a couple of these were placed together, and now stand for forest 林

A mouth 口 in a door 門 conveys the idea of asking, thus 問

Not only is the Chinese language almost unique as regards the formation of its written characters, but the vast number of words which can be formed from the same radical or root is extraordinary. The number of words in the language amounts to over forty thousand, but only a very small proportion of these are known to any but the *literati* of the empire.

The difficulty of the spoken language arises from the various tones, the meaning of a word varying according to the intonation of the voice, and sometimes having as many as fifteen different signi-fications.

To give an example of this, the word *che*, pronounced in exactly the same tone of voice, and without an aspirate, has eighteen different meanings. Among other things, it stands for our English nouns—famine, fowl, impediment, footprint, foundation, sieve, and small table, and is also used in expressing each and all of the following actions : to wind silk, to ridicule, to crowd, to draw water, to strike, and to investigate.

The same word, pronounced in exactly the same tone, but with an aspirate, has as many as ten different meanings. Among others, it stands for whispers, grief, cold, seven, wife ; and for the verbs to insult, to roost, to varnish, and to deceive.

Many absurd blunders are constantly made by foreign students of the Chinese language ; and we hear a man talking about his wives when he means to speak of his fowls ; calling for a cake, and having a bottle brought to him ; and making allusion to his nose when he wishes to talk about leather. In each of these cases the difference is merely the sounding or dropping of an aspirate.

Then we hear a bewildered servant being asked to serve his master with a soldier instead of a biscuit ; and a gentleman imagining that he is calling for his hat, when all the time he is asking for the cat ; and making remarks about a field which can only apply to heaven.

These are some of the pitfalls into which the outer barbarian falls when making his first attempts at conversation in the language of the Flowery Land. No wonder that he occasionally envies the gift of speech possessed by the chattering little Celestials playing in the streets !

Having spoken of the difficulties of the language our young China-man has to speak and write, let us look over his shoulder, and see what books he is studying. The first of all is the *San-Tsz-King*, or " Trimetrical Classic," because, to make it more easily remembered, it is written in lines of three words each. The teacher repeats the first few lines, and the scholars, holding their books in their hands, and swinging their small bodies backwards and forwards, follow his pronunciation of the words. They then return to their seats and commit the words to memory. In order to be sure each small boy is attending to his lessons, he is expected to shout out the passage he is learning at the top of his voice. The continual din caused by this arrangement can be better imagined than described; and when you pass a school-house in China, you are more likely to suspect the existence of Bedlam than of a place of learning.

The first sentence in the Chinese boys' primer runs as follows :— "Men at their birth are by nature radically good." The importance of study is then enlarged upon, and a sentence occurs to the effect that " To educate without severity shows a teacher's indolence." The sight of the bamboo rod, which is found in every school-room close to the master's hand, and in very constant use, is a proof that this maxim of the sage of old commends itself to the teachers of the present day. Chinese boys then go on to learn that there are three great powers— Heaven, earth, and man ; that there are three lights—the sun, moon, and stars. They are further informed that rice, millet, pulse, wheat, rye, and barley are the six kinds of grain on which men subsist. Various other matters of a similar kind are touched upon, followed by a summary of Chinese history. Afterwards, the example of sages and prodigies of past ages is commended to the notice of the youthful pupils. I will mention a few of these eminent examples of devotion to literature in olden times.

One celebrated student, Sun King by name, lived more than two thousand years ago, when the dynasty of Chau held sway in China. So enthusiastic was his devotion to study that he constantly shut himself up in his private apartments, and, lest he should be overcome by drowsiness, he fastened the hair of his head by a cord to a beam in the roof.

Another eminent scholar, whose family was poor, studied by the light from a number of glow-worms he had collected. And yet another conned his task by the light of the reflected snow. One committed his lesson to memory while bending beneath the weight of a load of faggots he carried on his back ; and yet another, whose thirst for knowledge could be controlled by no difficulties, fastened his book to the horns of one of the cows he was tending.

One "pattern of industry" took up his abode in the fastnesses of a celebrated mountain to study for his first degree. It was his custom to cast all family letters aside unopened, when he had ascertained that the characters signifying peace and health appeared upon the cover. His motive in so doing was to keep his mind free from all distraction of outside matters. A boy at the age of seven is described as being in all his conduct most dignified and decorous. He always used a round piece of wood for his pillow, so that he could awake easily and apply himself diligently to his studies. A second lad, who lived before the Christian era (for all these wonderful specimens of devotion to literature seem to have flourished in far-distant ages), was, although very poor, most anxious to become a scholar. He hit upon the device of boring a hole through the partition of his room to the house of his next-door neighbour. By the faint light from his friend's lamp, which struggled through the chink he had made, he pored over his books and became ultimately famous. At the age of seven, Wang Yu-ching could compose remarkable literary essays. He was the *protégé* of a certain assistant-prefect, who was charmed with his singular talents. One day this gentleman was dining with a friend, and the common Chinese entertainment of suggesting the first line of an impromptu stanza was introduced, the guests being invited to match the line. It was as follows : " The parrot though it talks cannot compare with the phœnix." None of the visitors were equal to the task, but upon returning home the assistant-prefect's little friend immediately suggested the admirable line—

"The spider though skilful cannot compare with the silk-worm."

Chinese boys know something of arithmetic and calculate very rapidly, but they do this with their little abacus, or counting-board.

Several other books are studied, and the classic of Filial Piety is largely used as a reading-book, and is more common in China than any "Boy's Own Paper " in England. Some of the stories it contains

give such graphic glimpses of Chinese life and character that I cannot
do better than relate a few of them for your amusement.

MANG TSUNG AND THE BAMBOO SHOOTS.

In days of old, during the dynasty of Chin, there lived a lad who
was called Mang Tsung. While still very young he had the misfortune
to lose his father. With a filial heart he constantly did reverence
before the carved tablet within which dwelt the spirit of his departed
sire. More than this, he devoted himself to the care of his
widowed mother, serving her with unwearying devotion and seeking
to supply her every want. Now it happened one day, in the
middle of winter, when the land was covered with a thin mantle
of snow, and trees were bare of leaves, that Mang's mother fell
ill, and would eat no food. Wearily she murmured, "If I could
but have a dish of the bamboo shoots which are found in the bright
spring-time, I would eat of them and be restored to strength again."
His mother's words pierced poor Mang Tsung's tender heart. He
desired that her every wish should be gratified; but how could the most
diligent seeker find young bamboo shoots in the depth of winter?
With a heavy heart the lad crept away from his old mother's side and
went out into the open street. He wandered along, scarce knowing
whither he went, till he came to the bamboo grove in the shadow of
an ancient temple. Falling full length upon the bare frozen earth,
he clasped his arms around the shining glossy stems of the graceful
bamboos, watering the ground meanwhile with his fast-falling tears,
when, lo! the bare wintry earth around the roots became loosened,
and was pierced by the tender white shoots of the young bamboos.
Joyfully Mang cut them down, and hurrying home, cooked and presented
the longed-for dainty to his sick mother.

Eagerly she partook of the dish procured for her by the devotion
of her son, and before she had finished the repast her strength
returned, and she was restored to health again. And so influenced
were heaven and earth by the pious conduct of this filial son, that
ever since the bamboos have continued to put forth their shoots in

the dull days of winter, instead of waiting for the awakening and vivifying influences of the spring.

LAO LAI-TSZ, OR THE FILIAL SON.

Long, long ago, at the time when the kings of the Chow dynasty ruled in China (three thousand years since), there lived a man whose name was Lao Lai-tsz. He had attained to the age of seventy, but since his venerable parents were still alive, he always declared that he was not old, and refused to be addressed by the title " Venerable " or " Ancient." His one desire in life seemed to be to make his beloved relatives forgetful of the flight of time, and to fill their hearts with mirth and gladness. He provided for them the daintiest of dishes, and served them day and night with unwearying devotion. Very often he would dress himself in a coat of many colours, just as if he were once more a child. Then he would dance and play before the old people, holding in his hands the toys of his infancy. Now and then he would go to the well and bring back a pail of clear water. Entering the guest room he would stumble like a child upon the threshold, and, falling upon the floor, pretend to cry piteously. Then running up to his old parents' side, he would beg to be comforted by them as in the days of his childhood. All this was done by Lao Lai-tsz with the noble object of gratifying and amusing his venerable relatives, and making them forget, for a time at least, their great age, and imagine that they were once more the youthful parents of a little child.

THE REWARD OF KOH KÜ.

In the time of the dynasty of Han there lived a man whose name was Koh Kü. His aged mother was sheltered beneath his roof, and he and his wife were the parents of a fine boy three years of age. Very happily they lived together, till adversity like a dark cloud brooded over the little family, and the father's labour could barely maintain them. Day by day the ancient dame shared with her little grandson her scanty meal. The cruel hand of famine rested upon them, their faces grew thin, and their strength failed. Then one day Koh Kü called to his wife to bring out the child and follow him. Shouldering his spade, he hastened on beyond the bamboo fence which bounded their small homestead, and coming to a standstill, he addressed his wife in the following words: "I have, alas, become so poor as to be unable to support my mother, and the child is constantly sharing the small portion of its grandmother, while both are growing weaker before our eyes. Another child may possibly be born to us, but a mother once dead can never return again. Let us bury the child, so that we may have sufficient for the maintenance of my mother."

The terrified wife was silent with fear; she dare not dispute her husband's will, but held the little one pressed closely to her bosom, while the husband dug the grave of his living child. Suddenly she heard a dull tinkling sound as the spade struck against some hard substance. It was followed by an exclamation of joy, and she soon saw her husband lifting some object out of the half-dug grave. It was a pot of gold, and it bore the following inscription: "Heaven bestows this treasure upon the dutiful son, Koh Kü. The magistrates must not claim it, neither must his neighbours attempt to take it from him."

In such a signal manner did Heaven reward the filial son, who valued so lightly the life of his child in comparison with the well-being of his aged mother.

THE IMAGES THAT WEPT.

Ting Lan was a man who lived in the days of the Han dynasty. His parents both died while he was still an infant, so that he was unable to repay them in the smallest degree for all their love and care. He was always longing to discover some way in which he could make his departed parents conscious of his deep devotion. One day he was seized with an inspiration, and taking up a piece of fragrant wood, he carved out of it the figures of his deceased parents, and henceforth tried to satisfy his loving heart by constantly watching and tending them as if they were indeed the forms of his beloved relatives

E

Now it happened that Ting Lan's wife was a woman who had little sympathy with him in his filial devotion ; in fact, she often made fun of him, refusing to do reverence before the images, or to take her share in waiting upon them. At last a day came when Ting Lan was absent from home, and it occurred to his wife that she would amuse herself by pricking the wooden hands of the images with her needle. When, behold, drops of blood were seen to flow from the scars she had made, and soon after, upon the return of her husband, he discovered that tears were falling from their eyes. He investigated the cause of their grief, and upon discovering it, this filial son divorced his irreverent wife, sending her away from his home for ever.

THE STORY OF WANG LIANG.

In the far-away time of the dynasty of Chin, there lived a boy whose name was Wang Liang. When he was very young he had the misfortune to lose his mother. His father soon afterwards married a woman whose name was Chu. This new wife was of a scolding and unamiable disposition, and she took a violent dislike to her small step-son. Daily and hourly she had some fault to find with him, and was always complaining of him to his father. Wang Liang felt this to be the unkindest cut of all, since even his father's approval was no longer his. At length a day came when the sky was dull and leaden, while the streets and roofs of the houses were white with fallen snow. Not only were the little icicles hanging from the curled eaves of the houses, but pond and lake and river were alike covered with a thick sheet of ice. Mrs. Wang had enlivened the dull hours of the short winter's day with ceaseless complaints, till at last, throwing herself down on her stiff-backed chair, and warming her arms with the small hand-stove which was hidden away in her capacious sleeves, she exclaimed, " Would that I had a dish of carp fresh from the lake ! "

Now that was an extremely foolish desire for Mrs. Wang to give expression to, since with every piece of water for miles around covered with ice, how was it possible for any one to obtain fresh fish ? But her step-son, who had listened silently to her exclamation, crept quietly out of the room, and slipping on his bright-coloured wind-cap and thrusting his small hands up into his long sleeves, he hurried along to the river-side.

It stretched away before him in the silent moonlight, a plain of ice dusted with powdery snow.

Hastily he cast aside his garments till he was all exposed to the keen blast of the wild winter wind. Then he threw himself down on the unyielding ice, in the hope that the warmth from his small shivering body would melt it away beneath him. Upon such filial devotion as this Heaven will always smile; and the thick sheet of ice was made to melt away beneath the dutiful lad, and two fine carp leaped out from the dark-flowing stream. They were joyfully seized by the lad's ready hand, and hastily attiring himself he made his way to his father's house.

Kneeling at the feet of his unamiable step-mother, while he knocked his head to the ground, he presented her with the fish for which she had apparently so vainly longed.

The little book from which these stories are extracted is known by the title of the *Twenty-four Examples of Filial Piety*. Each story is illustrated with a wood-cut representing the hero engaged in performing his special act of filial piety. There is little doubt that the incidents recorded in this small volume, and accepted by the Chinese as historical facts, have been in no small degree influential in forming the characters of China's rising generation. A favourite Chinese proverb teaches that "Of the hundred virtues the chief is filial piety,"—and no other duty is so carefully and constantly instilled into the children's minds as this.

CHAPTER V.

CHINESE BOYS AT PLAY.

But what about the life of these little Chinamen and Chinawomen when school work is over and lessons done? Surely, though they are dressed in clothing of the same pattern as their grandfathers and grandmothers, and have such wonderful memories for their extremely dry and uninteresting lessons, they must occasionally find time for a romp or game of some sort, or they would not be boys and girls at all. This is perfectly true; and though the Chinese boys have no cricket or football, no marbles or hockey, and understand nothing of paper-chases and boating, they are not without some amusements; and even if they are a trifle more old-fashioned and sober than English children, yet they enjoy their games quite as heartily.

Kite-flying is the great delight of Chinese boys, though not of boys alone, but also of their fathers and grandfathers. And what famous kites they have too! Some are in the form of beautiful birds, or butterflies, with wings cleaving the air; others are in the shape of men, or various animals, dragons, and centipedes. Occasionally a tiny paper lantern is fastened to the tail of a kite, and being lighted it has a very pretty effect as it rises, shining like a star in the twilight. Sometimes a number of bird-kites are fastened by short lines to the principal cord, and when flying in the air look like a flight of birds clustering round one common centre.

The great day for the commencement of kite-flying is the ninth of the ninth moon; and the selection of this particular day has, like most things in China, a superstitious origin. "Once upon a time," they say, "in the far-away ages of the past, a man was warned that on a certain day a great calamity would befall him and his. When the time came round, the man, with every member of his household, decided to leave home and spend the day in the country, among the hills. Upon returning at nightfall he found that all his domestic animals were dead. The day was the ninth of the ninth month; and ever since, people have been careful to absent themselves from home on that singularly inauspicious day; and in order to enliven the time they amuse themselves by flying kites."

Then there are the lanterns of all sizes and shapes, which are the pride of the first month of the year. Gay indeed are the streets of a Chinese city from the tenth to the fifteenth of the first moon; for though most of the shops are closed, and all other business suspended for nearly a fortnight, the lantern-sellers do a brisk trade. Chinese ingenuity is taxed to find new shapes for these lanterns. The salesmen, with their wares attached to long bamboo poles, take up their positions outside the closed shop fronts, and the streets are so crowded with spectators and buyers that it is very difficult to make one's way along.

Most of the lanterns are made of bright-coloured paper, over a light bamboo framework. Some are made in the shape of a ball fixed to the end of a stick, others are like rabbits, horses or fowls, and are mounted on wheels. Some are in the form of shrimps, crabs or beetles; others are representations of favourite flowers, such as the lotus and camellia. A large number are made of light gauze or silk, and have mythological or historical scenes painted upon them. But the most expensive of all contain wheels and fine wires, which are made to revolve by the heated air inside when the lantern is lighted. The small figures on the outside, to whose heads, legs or arms the wires are attached, then begin to move, and we see, here an old man fishing, there a ferryman rowing across a stream, and here, again, two Chinese gentlemen exchanging New Year's greetings.

When Chinese children want more active amusements, they play battledore and shuttlecock, only the battledore is usually the thick sole of the shoe, or the instep of the foot. They manage them so cleverly that it is quite common to see the shuttlecock struck some two or three hundred times without a single miss.

Ta chiau, or "hitting the ball," is another favourite game. English boys would no doubt consider it rather monotonous, since it is simply played by striking the ball to the ground with the hand as many times as possible.

Ta teh-lo is "whipping the top." A Chinese top is made of bamboo, with a piece of wood going through it, and a large hole is cut in the side, which makes it have a fine humming sound as it spins. "Hiding from the cat" is not unlike our English "blind man's buff;" one child having his eyes blinded, and trying to catch the others, who escape from him in all directions.

"Catching shrimps" is another game, in which all the boys have their eyes covered, and try to catch each other. Ta pan is not unlike hopscotch. Every child has a small flat stone or copper cash, and standing on a marked line, tries to strike the stone which has been thrown by the first boy.

"Turning the dragon" is the favourite amusement of Chinese boys in the spring time; and, like most of their pleasures, it has a religious or superstitious signification. The passage of this fabulous animal through the streets of their cities is believed to be very effectual in dispelling all evil influences, especially a tendency to various sicknesses thought to exist in the first month of the year.

The body of the dragon is composed of a large number of lanterns fastened together, and covered with coloured paper and cloth. It is frequently thirty or forty feet long. The numerous joints of which it is composed make it capable of being twisted and turned in all directions, and its formidable-looking head and wagging tail make it indeed a striking object.

Long poles are attached to a number of the joints, and in the evening it is brightly lighted up. As the many-jointed creature is carried through the streets, turning and twisting in all directions, rearing its ill-favoured head and gaping mouth, it is pursued by immense crowds of people. The procession accompanying it makes a

THE PUNCH AND JUDY SHOW.

most unearthly din, beating gongs, and letting off squibs and crackers, to the great amazement of the Western stranger who for the first time looks upon the singular spectacle.

Another game somewhat similar to this is described as the "Lion playing with the ball." The lion is made in very much the same way as the dragon, and is carried by two men or boys. Poles are not usually employed, as in carrying the dragon ; but the boys insert their heads n the body of the monster, while their figures and legs are dressed to represent the imaginary legs of the animal. This representation of the king of beasts is made with gaping jaws, which are a great convenience to the persons who put themselves in the position of his legs and feet, since they can see through the opening what is going on. The Chinese have an idea that the lion is very fond of playing with a ball, and accordingly a boy walks in front of the procession carrying a very large one. This young hopeful darts across the lion's path, running hither and thither to his heart's content; and wherever the ball is seen the lion follows, causing great amusement not only to the boys who take part in the procession, but to the spectators who crowd the streets.

The performances of the Punch and Judy shows are much appreciated by Chinese children, and many people are inclined to believe they were introduced into England from China. In any case, they were well known in that empire many hundreds of years ago.

As for the pets kept by Chinese boys, some of them are identical with those which are prized by English children—such as rabbits, kittens, and gold fish. Crickets are also very largely kept by boys, as well as older people. Chinamen are so fond of gambling that it is no wonder we should see the children imitating their fathers, and the boys are very fond of placing two of these insects in a bowl or deep dish, and irritating them with a straw or stick till they begin to fight desperately, each boy risking the few cash he may possess on the chance of the cricket he selects being the winner of the fight.

They have many favourite birds, among others the canary and lark, and one very much prized is a sort of thrush, called the "bird

A CRICKET FIGHT.

with the flowery eyebrow." You may often see the boys walking
on the city walls or other open spaces, carrying their caged birds
out for an airing. Another little creature which affords them
much amusement is the cicada, which they capture in the early
summer time, while he sings his hoarse song on the flower stalks or
among the bushes. The poor insect is confined in a tiny cage of
bamboo, and is occasionally poked up by his juvenile owner, to drone
out as hoarse and unmusical a ditty as ever he chirruped in the days
of his freedom. Hedgehogs and tortoises are also kept as pets : the
latter is believed to attain to a great age, and is used, with the stork, as
an emblem of longevity.

Few Chinese toys are of a durable nature. There are not many
toy shops, but cheap playthings are sold by an itinerant vendor of
small wares, whose approach is announced by the beating of a gong,
which calls the children as quickly out of the houses as the music
of Hamelin's Pied Piper is said to have done. They gather in
crowds round his baskets loaded with clay or pasteboard figures.
Here are cages with miniature birds in them ; ladies riding on non-
descript animals supposed to represent mules ; carts carrying a drum
which beats as the wheels revolve. Figures of genii and idols abound ;
and now and then an extraordinary figure is seen, whose light-
coloured locks, tight-fitting clothing, and the stick carried in the
hand, proclaim it to be intended for a "foreign barbarian."

Most Chinese children are possessed of the proverbial "sweet
tooth," and the demand for sugar-candy and sweetmeats is very
liberally supplied. The whole stock-in-trade of the Chinese confec-
tioner is often carried in two baskets suspended on a pole from the
man's shoulders. One basket contains the pots, pans, and other
utensils necessary for the prosecution of his trade ; the other a
tempting array of sweets of all shapes and sizes. Some are of various
bright colours and curious shapes, and many contain morsels of
ground nuts or walnuts. In front of these sugar stalls a revolving
pointer is often seen, a circle of barley-sugar being ranged beneath
it. Few Chinese boys are able to resist the temptation of paying

down their cash for a turn at the wheel, in the hope that they may gain two or three sticks for their money instead of one.

Nuts also are in great demand among Chinese schoolboys. Beside walnuts and ground-nuts, they have water-nuts, and are fond of melon and sunflower seeds; while small pieces of sugar-cane, sold at the rate of one twentieth part of a penny each, are eagerly bought up. So you see that Chinese boys are not unlike English children in enjoying a good game of play, and they also very highly appreciate the sweetmeats upon which so many pennies are spent with so much satisfaction in our own land.

The difference between Chinese and English boys lies in

ITINERANT TOYMAN.

the fact that with us active sports requiring physical exertion are commended; whereas in China all violent exercise is discouraged, and a boy is taught that the more dignified and grave his

deportment, the greater approbation will he receive from his elders.

Chinese boys are fond of asking riddles, and some of the juvenile prodigies of ancient days are represented as having been very clever in composing these enigmas. Many of them it is not possible to give in English, because they are puns upon Chinese words; and others relate to some peculiarity in the way in which a character is written, or to some resemblance it bears to another character with a different meaning.

I will give two of the latter :—

"A joking Siu-ts'ai, or Bachelor of Arts, asked a Buddhist priest (who as a class are usually ignorant), ' How do you write "bald pate ?"'' alluding to the shaven head which is the distinctive mark of the Buddhist priesthood.

ITINERANT SELLER OF SWEETMEATS.

"'That is quite easy,' was the unexpected reply. 'I take the Bachelor of Art's tail and turn it round.'"

秀　Bachelor of Arts.　　秃　Bald-head.

Another, somewhat similar in form to many popular English riddles, is the following:

"What is that which raises its head in embarrassment and lowers it in wealth?"

The character 田. In wealth 富 it is at the foot, in embarrassment 累 at the head of the character of which it forms a part.

Others of a different kind are more readily understood in England, so I will mention several.

"What is the fire that has no smoke, and the water that has no fish?"

"A glow-worm's fire has no smoke, and well-water has no fish."

"Mention the name of an object with two mouths, which travels by night and not by day."

"A lantern."

"What is that of which we have too much, and that of which we desire more?"

"A summer day is too long (on account of the great heat), and we wish a winter day were longer."

"What are the eyes of Heaven, the bones of water, and the looking-glass of the sky?"

The answers are, "Stars, ice, and the sea."

"What is it that has a gaping mouth, and marches on like an invading army, devouring at every step?"

"A pair of scissors cutting cloth."

The amusement of solving riddles is so popular in China among all classes, that at the time of the Feast of Lanterns you may often see a group of literary men, as well as the common people, gathered round a doorway, over which hangs a lantern upon which several enigmas are written.

Prizes varying from several hundreds of cash to some trifling gift of nuts, sweetmeats, etc., are offered for the correct solution of these riddles, and crowds of people collect and engage in eager competition, rather on account of the sport afforded than for the value of the prize offered.

A CHINESE LANTERN AND BEARER.

CHAPTER VI.

CHINESE GIRLS AT HOME.

IF you were to ask a Chinaman how many children he had in his family, he would reply by telling you the number of his sons. The girls among them are not counted : why should such worthless little beings be reckoned in with their ever-welcome eagerly-desired brothers?

"A boy is worth ten times as much as a girl"; and, "If a girl does no harm, it is enough : you cannot expect her to be either useful or good," are two of the common sayings of which I could quote many to show you how lightly the daughters of China are valued.

How I wish the girls of England would think sometimes of their little sisters in far-off China! Girls looking back to a childhood all unlike that of England's happy daughters, to a future more different still.

Let us take a peep into some of these Chinese homes both of the richer and the poorer classes, and try and find out the sort of life the girls live, and why they are thought so little of.

One reason for the universal feeling that girls are useless burdens is hinted at in the Chinese proverb, "A daughter is like a fine young bamboo springing up just outside your garden fence." That is, the child may be fair and lovable, but she does not belong to you: as soon as she is old enough to repay a parent's care, she goes off into another family, and is rarely if ever seen by her own relatives.

Girls in China are married, or taken into the family of the little boy to whom they are betrothed, at such an early age that their parents see very little of them after the years of childhood are past.

But a stronger reason than this lies in the fact of the disappointment that parents feel when for the first time a baby-girl opens her eyes upon the strange new world, and takes the place, as it seems to them, of the boy they would have been so glad to welcome. And why, you will ask, do they value their sons so much? Principally, perhaps, because the more sons they have the more important people will they be—since these sons will not only always remain under their father's roof, but young wives will be brought there, and families grow up in the same house. A man with many sons becomes before long a person of importance.

Besides this, it is believed that when a man dies and passes into the unseen world he needs food and clothing and money, just as he did while on earth. The Chinese profess to have found out a plan for supplying a dead man with all he needs. Paper money, paper garments, paper houses, furniture and servants are all burned, and are thus transmitted into the world beyond the grave. And only boys can render this service to their parents. If a family consists of girls only, then no one will be able to worship and burn incense before the spirit tablet which will be set up in the home of the departed when they die, which one of their spirits is supposed to enter. For a Chinaman believes he has three souls, and at death one is buried with the body, another enters the unseen world, the third dwells in the tablet. The hungry unclothed spirits of those who leave behind them no sons to attend to their wants, will wander destitute and homeless in the dim regions of the spirit world. Is it wonderful, when they believe this, that girls are despised and lightly valued by the Chinese, while boys are highly prized and fondly loved?

Sometimes soon after a little girl is born her father will call in a blind fortune-teller, who is supposed to know all about the future. These men are constantly seen going up and down Chinese streets beating on the little gong they carry in their hands to let people know they are coming. When the fortune-teller is questioned about the little girl, and told the year, month, day and hour of her birth, he makes a calculation, and perhaps tells them that their little daughter will be very unfortunate all through life; she has been born under a very unlucky star, and nothing she does will prosper. Then the parents think, if their child is likely to be so unfortunate, they had better at once give her to some nuns, to be brought up by them, since then she will at least never want for food or clothing. These child nuns are taught by the older inhabitants of the nunnery to weave and embroider, and not unfrequently to read and write. They serve the elder devotees and assist in the temple services, and on the whole their lot is less hard than that of many Chinese girls in their own homes.

Sometimes the fortune-teller says that the little girl's fate is bad : not only will she be unfortunate, but if they keep her in the house she will be the cause of harm to her friends; worst of all, her brother may very likely die. Perhaps he was born in a year of the cycle named " Hare," and if she were born on a day of the cycle of the " Dog," then her influence will certainly prove fatal to him, unless she be removed, since hares are destroyed by dogs. In this case the little girl will probably be given away to some woman who is willing to take and bring up a child as the future wife of her little son. It is considered necessary that an arrangement of this kind should be closed by money, and a sum no larger than a shilling is not unfrequently given, because such little girls are thought to be worth nothing. " Is that your daughter? " I have sometimes asked a Chinese woman, as I have seen a little girl sitting by her side. " No, she is betrothed to my son," is a frequent reply, as she looks away to a small boy playing merrily, with his thoughts more exercised by the making of mud-pies than anything else.

If a girl is blind or lame, her chances of life are small.

One child, whom I knew well, was lame, and her family determined to get rid of her, so they carried her to the gate of the Mission compound, and left her there, to see if the " Jesus teachers " cared to take her. How glad she was when she was taken in, dressed in comfortable clothing, fed, and kindly spoken to ! How eagerly she listened to the sweet story of Jesus and His love ; of how He made the lame to walk, and placed His hands on little children's heads, and loves them still—girls even, as well as boys !

You can guess how pleased the missionaries were when, years after, they used to hear the little lame girl telling to new arrivals in the school the joyful Gospel news which had made her own heart glad. She has gone home now to the mansions prepared for Chinese as well as English children. I think she often felt very thankful she was lame, even though she suffered severe pain at times, for if she had been strong and well her parents might never have laid her down at the missionaries' gate, and, like many millions of Chinese children, she might have died without hearing of the Lord Jesus.

What do these Chinese girls look like ? you may ask. Well, many of them have bright, attractive faces, and all have very dark eyes. They wear their raven locks dressed in different ways, according to the province in which they live. In most parts the hair is drawn back and twisted into one heavy strand, which hangs down the back, and is tied with scarlet cord. Frequently the front hair is cut, making a fringe similar to an English fashion. Sometimes two plaits are made and bunched up at either side of the head, being decorated with gaily-coloured flowers. At other times, especially in the winter season, they wear a strange little head-dress, consisting of a silken embroidered band, with a thick black silk fringe hanging down over the forehead and ears. When a girl is about thirteen years of age her hair is put up in womanly style. It is twisted round curious wire frames of various shapes. Some are like butterflies' wings, others resemble a teapot handle. Other young ladies wear enormous chignons, and Manchu girls have their hair tied in a large bow upon the top of their heads. Until their marriage most girls wear the hair in front dressed round, keeping the natural appearance of the forehead. After the wedding it is dressed square. This appearance is obtained by pulling out the hairs round the forehead, making it look broad and high. Even little girls frequently wear heavy earrings, bracelets and rings, if they belong to a rich family.

When in holiday attire, most girls have their cheeks adorned with rouge, and a little touch of it just under the lower lip. They also use white powder very plentifully.

A Chinese girl is very little troubled with considerations of fashion. It is true there is a slight difference in the cut of the garments worn by girls and women of different provinces. Most frequently the more costly tunics and embroidered skirts descend from the grandmother down to several generations of her grandchildren. It is true that certain shades in the colour of material are in greater favour one year than another; that the width of the sleeves and the style of trimming does, to some extent, vary, but by no means in the degree that is found in Western lands.

In summer the underclothing of the middle and upper classes is usually composed of fine grass-cloth; in winter, of cotton-cloth. The outer garments are all of the same shape, but differ much in material and colour. In summer the loose tunic or pelisse is often made of beautiful silky Chinese gauze, and will be in colour light blue, green, or grey. The trousers or pantalettes are frequently of the same material, of a different colour, and you will often see red silk trousers with a green tunic, and purple gauze trousers with a pelisse of figured blue silk. These gorgeous garments are trimmed with gold braid, intermixed with silk of various shades, and the large sleeves of the best tunics are trimmed with broad strips of satin, embroidered with fairy landscapes, or birds and flowers.

But the most important part of a young girl's dress in China is her shoes. Such tiny shoes they are, of coloured silk or satin, most tastefully embroidered, with brightly painted heels, just peeping beneath the neat pantalette; and the feet are supposed to merit the poetical name bestowed upon them of "golden lilies." But how sad it is to discover that such a result is produced by indescribable torture, and that the part of the foot which is not seen is nothing but a mass of distorted or broken bones!

This deformity is produced, not by iron or wooden shoes, as is sometimes supposed, but by narrow cotton bandages about three yards long. They are applied when the little girl is six years old.

One end of the strip of cotton is placed beneath the instep and then carried over the four small toes, drawing them down beneath the foot. Another twist draws the heel and great toe nearer together, making an indentation beneath the sole. When all the cloth has been used, the end is firmly sewed down, and the feet are left for a week or two in that condition. Clean bandages are now and then put on, but the change has to be very rapidly effected, or the blood begins again to circulate in the poor benumbed feet, and the agony becomes almost unbearable. Not unfrequently during the process a girl loses one or two of her toes; but she feels repaid for the pain she endures by being the possessor of still smaller feet. Mothers and nurses frequently perform this duty for their daughters, and in passing a Chinese home one sometimes hears the bitter crying of a child whose feet are being bound.

Yet so strong is the power of fashion that sooner than be unlike other girls, or have to bear the derision of their neighbours, who will laugh at them and say, "Just look at those two boats going by," in reference to their large feet, they prefer to endure the pain. I have known cases of little girls, whose parents had been induced by the missionaries to refrain from binding their feet, who would actually procure bandages and try to do the binding themselves.

For the first year or so the children suffer constant pain. By numberless devices they try to benumb the feet and relieve agony. Through the weary summer days they lie restless with fever upon the cool mats of their couch, and when the cold nights of winter come they are afraid to wrap themselves in any covering, since if the limbs grow warm the suffering becomes more intense. When the feet are first bound it is very difficult to use them. Girls can only move about by means of two stools, upon which they rest their knees and which are moved alternately by their hands. At last this much desired smallness is obtained, the girl's foot is deformed for life, and she is greatly admired by all her friends.

"What a good mother she must have had!" is a remark frequently made when a girl is seen with smaller feet than usual.

"Ah," said a Chinese mother to me, who was grieving over the death of her daughter, " she was a grown-up girl. Had she been little, I should not have minded at all; and she had the tiniest of tiny feet." Not, Is she good, or clever, or beautiful? do the guests ask at a Chinese wedding—but, What is the size of her foot?

Three inches is the correct length of the fashionable shoes in which Chinese ladies toddle and limp, supporting themselves on a child's shoulder, or by means of a strong staff. Some very wealthy ladies are the possessors of feet which are almost useless, and as they can hardly walk from one room to another in their spacious mansions they are not unfrequently carried, especially about their gardens, on the backs of their large-footed attendants. Women whose feet are not quite so small, though still tightly bound, manage to walk occasionally, with great difficulty, a distance of several miles. "Their movements are as the waving of the willows," says a Chinese poet in reference to those tiny feet; but to English eyes the gait appears to be by no means elegant, and bears a strong resemblance to what would be obtained by walking on our heels.

This custom has no connection with religion, and is not prescribed by the law of the country. Indeed, no small-footed woman is allowed within the precincts of the Imperial Palace, and no Manchu woman binds her feet. It is only the spread of Christianity, and the growing up of that Christian public feeling, which teaches compassion for the weak, and sympathetic tenderness for the suffering, that can abolish foot-binding from Chinese homes.

Slowly, but surely, this influence is already working, and in connection with several of our native churches anti-footbinding societies have been formed. These are joined, not only by the guardians of young girls, but by the parents of lads. For only when people become willing that their sons should marry large-footed wives, can there be any widespread ceasing from bandaging in China. "I shall never bind the feet of my daughters, or allow them to marry any one but a Christian," says many a Chinese Christian to-day. And they keep to this resolution, in very many cases in the midst of persecution and suffering, and surrounded on all sides by trials and difficulties, we in England know little of.

The origin of this custom of footbinding seems very doubtful. It is sometimes referred back to an empress of an ancient dynasty, who bound her feet, some say to hide a deformity, and others to make them more beautifully small. Some accounts declare it was introduced with the idea of preventing women from going much from home. The

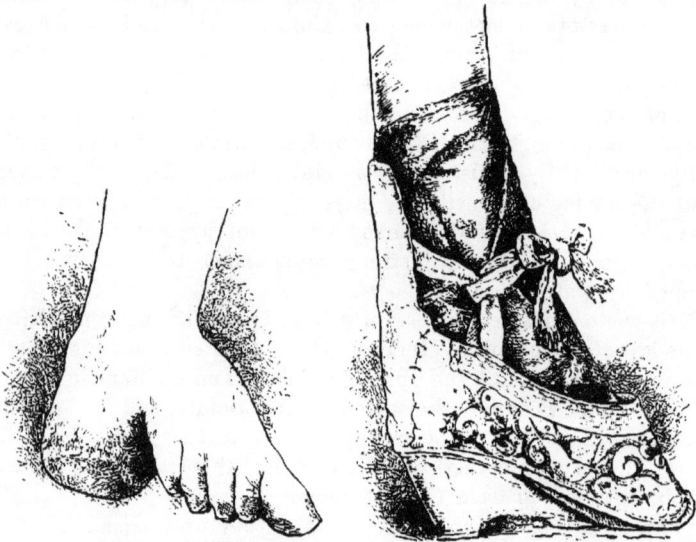

GOLDEN LILIES—BARE AND SHOD.

Chinese think if young girls go out of doors they are sure to get into mischief; and in one book the example of an eminent lady of olden times is commended to their notice, who " for twelve years never looked out of the door of her house."

Girls of the wealthier classes are seldom seen abroad, but the daughters of the poor lead a much freer and happier life. When little more than babies, and just able to carry a basket and rake, they are sent out on the city wall, to a piece of waste land, or the slope of some neighbouring hill to collect fuel for the family.

They gather the dry grass and sticks, and scrape together the fallen needles of the pine trees, and everything else that can possibly be used in keeping up the fire, which is lighted only for cooking purposes. The Chinese are not usually particularly unkind to little children, and they need only fear a beating if they fail to gather sufficient fuel to keep the pot boiling. In the bright spring-time, when the fresh wild herbs are springing up over the waste places and on the slopes of the city wall, the children may be seen filling their baskets, and making in this way a small addition to the family meal.

While still very tiny children, girls are intrusted with the care of the baby. The little one frequently sits on his small sister's back in a scarf which is tied over her shoulders. The baby's feet dangle at her side, his arms are often round her neck, and his small head bobs up and down as she runs about, or sways herself from side to side to quiet him.

Little girls also find very pleasant employment during the cotton harvest in picking the snowy balls. They take care of the silkworms, too, gathering mulberry-leaves to feed them upon, till they spin the beautiful balls of delicate floss silk, that are woven into the costly plain and flowered fabrics for which China is so justly famous.

Nearly all the girls are taught to assist their mothers in spinning and weaving the cotton cloth required for the family garments. They also learn to cook the simple meals of rice and sweet potato, or various other vegetables and fish, meat being very rarely indeed within their reach.

Many little girls, while very young, are able to add their mite to the family income by learning under their mother's direction one of the numberless small trades which employ the busy fingers of poor Chinese women.

A large number of children are taught to make the soles which are used for Chinese shoes. They paste pieces of old rag on a board or shutter till a thickness of about half an inch is obtained. The substance is then dried in the sun, and, after being stripped from the board, is ready for the shoemaker's use. Others for a short season are employed in the manufacture of the beautiful lanterns, of all shapes and sizes, which are in such universal request during the festivities of the first month of the year. In Central China also one is often reminded of the lacemaking districts of England by seeing girls seated at pillows and turning over bobbins, which are almost identical with those which Cowper saw in his Buckinghamshire village, and wrote—

> "Yon cottager, who weaves at her own door,
> Pillow and bobbins all her little store;
> Content though mean, and cheerful if not gay,
> Shuffling her threads about the livelong day."

When will the day come when we shall be able to add of these busy Chinese workers :—

> "Just knows, and knows no more, her Bible true,
> And in that charter reads, with sparkling eyes,
> Her title to a treasure in the skies"?

Other girls are skilful in making small paper boxes used in jewellers' shops, and many are employed in the plaiting of silk to lengthen queues.

The art of embroidering also supplies work to a large number of women and girls. At a very early age the children are taught to assist in their mother's business, and many little girls are kept so closely to their frames that their eyes are permanently injured. The shoe and fancy shops give out a large quantity of work to these busy toilers, but the wages paid for it are very low.

In many cases, for common embroidery not more than threepence a day is paid. For the finer work, whose delicate beauty excites the admiration of all English ladies, they never receive more than eight-pence or ninepence a day, working from early dawn till dusk. But the industry which employs probably a far larger number of girls than any other is that of making paper money, to be used in the worship of the gods, and of deceased relatives. Much that is used for this purpose consists merely of thin perforated Chinese paper. But the more elaborate paper money, in the making of which the small hands of children are engaged, takes the form of ingots, similar in appearance to the shoes or lumps of silver used in all large trading transactions. In their manufacture strips of thick paper are twisted into forms bearing a resemblance to the real ingots, and scraps of gilt paper or tinfoil are then pasted on them. They are strung in rows of twenty or more, and represent a considerable amount of money in the supposed currency of the spirit-world.

Not unfrequently girls of the poorer classes are sold as slaves to wealthy ladies. The sums paid for them vary, but frequently do not exceed five pounds. They are usually employed in the care of their mistresses' children, and are often not unkindly treated. But sometimes the mistress is possessed of a violent temper, and will half starve and mercilessly beat her little slave for the smallest misdemeanours; and then their lot is hard indeed.

One little slave girl in Hankow had been so cruelly beaten by her mistress, who only two years before had given the sum of forty pounds for her, that in despair she took a dose of opium, hoping thus to find in death an escape from her misery. She was only thirteen years of age. Her owners, when they discovered what she had done, tried several native remedies believed to be antidotes : among others they used the warm blood of a fowl just killed. But seeing no sign of recovery, they sent at last for a foreign missionary, having heard that Europeans were often able to restore those who were in the early stages of the opium stupor. When the missionary reached the residence of the little slave's owner, he found he had been summoned too late. He did all he could, but the unhappy little girl could not be restored.

Another little slave, whose mistress lived in the district ravaged recently by a great famine, made her escape in that time of general distress, and was brought by a relative to a Christian Mission school.

She was received by the missionaries, who were kept in ignorance of her former history. As time passed by she made good progress in her studies, and heard of One who gave His life that even little girls might be blessed. She was very happy in her new life, till a day came when, as not unfrequently occurred, some Chinese ladies asked permission to look over the school. It was observed that this little scholar seemed greatly terrified when she saw them, though she gave no reason for her very evident alarm. Some time after, the mystery was explained, when one of the ladies made a formal claim for the child, saying she was her slave who had escaped from her. The little scholar clung to her Christian teachers with tears and entreaties, begging them to allow her to remain with them. But the case was so clear, and the lady's claim so indisputable, that they could not refuse to restore her to her owner, although they did it with sorrowful hearts.

Another girl I knew had been purchased by a family in rather poor circumstances, to bring up as the betrothed of their eldest son. The boy died, and so the poor little girl was kept in the family as the drudge of the household. She never was called by any other name but that of ya-tou or "slave." She was only about ten years of age, but was ordered to carry almost constantly, upon her back, a child more than four years of age belonging to her mistress. She was not strong, and the constant carrying of a burden far too heavy for her developed hip disease, and the poor child became a constant sufferer. Her owners were so annoyed at her uselessness that they would do little to relieve her pain, and refused to allow her to enter the Mission Hospital. Some time after, the ladies in charge of a Mission boarding school succeeded in prevailing upon them to give her up to their care. As she was quite unable to do any work for her owners, they at last consented to this arrangement. So the little invalid has found a kind Christian home, and when I last heard of her she was somewhat improving in health.

Other girls are not sold, but pawned by their relatives, in seasons of poverty, and can be reclaimed when the small sum of money advanced upon them is repaid.

I have not yet touched upon the question of the education of Chinese girls, because, unless in very exceptional cases, they receive none. Sometimes a wealthy man will allow his little daughter to share in her brother's studies for a short time ; and the children who are brought up in the nunneries are, as I mentioned before, usually taught to read and write.

Most of the heroines of Chinese stories are able not only to read and write, but also to compose rhymes ending with given words—an accomplishment in high repute among Chinese students. But these talented young ladies appear much more frequently in the pages of Chinese story books than in real life ; and this not by any means because Chinese girls are wanting in intelligence, but because it is considered unwise to allow them to become as clever as their future husbands. Moreover, it is feared that if girls learn to read, they will be injured by the study of bad books ; since, according to a Chinese writer, "the feminine mind is unsteady in purpose and easily swerved from the right." Yet in past ages there have been now and again "bright particular stars" among the ranks of Chinese women, especially of the upper classes of society, who have tried to gain some insight into the literature of their country.

One of the most celebrated of these ladies was Pan Chao, who lived in the first century after Christ. She considered that it was desirable that girls should be educated, and so also did the Empress of Tai-Tsung, a ruler of the Tang dynasty. Another lady of high rank who lived at about the same period, spent much time and thought in arranging passages from the classics for the instruction of her niece, who was about to enter the imperial palace.

The several volumes which have been compiled for the use of Chinese girls are all very similar, and usually bear some such title as "Counsels," "Instructions," or "Admonitions for the Inner Apartments." Girls are there exhorted to pay close attention to all household duties, and particular directions are given as to the dress and manners becoming to young maidens. They are taught to be respectful to their elders, and very minute directions are given to guide them in their behaviour to their mother-in-law and their future husband. They are told to cultivate the " Four Virtues and Three Obediences." The former relate to correct manners, and include modesty and docility, careful speech, a submissive demeanour, and proper employment, literally "silk and thread," which refer to weaving and embroidering.

The " Three Obediences," or degrees of dependence, are that of a daughter upon her father, a wife upon her husband, and a mother upon her son. Some of the duties which are enlarged upon in these Chinese girls' primers would meet with approval even in the West. A girl is charged to be truthful, unselfish, and loving; to "be tranquil and reverent in the thoughts of the heart, and then the inner life will clearly manifest itself in the outward actions." She is counselled never to search out other people's affairs, like a busybody, and to treat her handmaids and slaves with forbearance and kindness. "Do not ferret out the smallest errors in accounts, and then beat the servants if they fall a cash or two short in the reckoning : you may think such conduct a proof of wisdom, but it rather exhibits your parsimony," is the counsel and verdict of one writer.

One of these books contains an account of an educated Chinese mother who trained her two sons most carefully, and read to them stories of the noble patriots and statesmen of their own country. In after life it is said these sons were known as wise, clean-handed officials, daring to refuse bribes and giving righteous judgment ; " which was certainly the result of their mother's teaching." I remember also when in 1882 the mother of the Viceroy Li Hung-chang, the greatest man in China to-day, died at Wuchang, a sort of memoir was issued by her sons, which contained a most interesting account of her early years, and attributed the honours and high rank to which her children had attained to her wise training and unceasing care.

These Chinese books to which I have referred frequently lay down rules relating to the toilette, and what girls should think of while making it. " Whilst powdering the face they should remember that the heart must be kept white and clean ; in arranging the head-dress, consider that the heart needs to be carefully regulated ; in oiling the hair, resolve to make the heart pliable and docile." Most of the girls of the upper classes are instructed in the art of cookery. They are commanded to imitate the example of a certain empress who always superintended the preparation of the dishes which appeared on the emperor's table. Another lady of rank, in days of old, always made it her practice to go into her kitchen at dawn of day and prepare gruel for her servants, ordering them to eat it before commencing their work.

Girls are also taught to show hospitality to strangers ; and, since example is always more forcible than precept, the story of an hospitable lady of olden times is related to them. This eminent dame, when her family were in very poor circumstances, sold her hair to purchase a meal for her guest, and emptied her pillow of straw to satisfy the hunger of his horse.

But these books find their way into the hands of very few Chinese girls, since, as I mentioned before, very few learn to read, and girls' schools, with the exception of those established by missionaries, are almost unknown.

After the age of eight or ten, the daughters of the wealthier classes are kept within the walls of their own homes. It is thought improper for them to be seen out of doors.

They have few amusements, and though they have not to endure the hard grinding poverty of the poorer classes, their life is much more cramped, and they have little variety in it.

Most of the larger houses have fine gardens attached to them, containing winding walks which pass under arches of curious rockwork, and over streams or ponds spanned by the well-known willow-pattern bridge. But the indoor life is very monotonous.

Some girls are taught to play on musical instruments, and to sing songs or selections from the classics, in a high unnatural key, by no means attractive to the ears of Europeans.

They spend much time in working embroidery. The paper patterns for these wonderful flowers, birds, and figures, which are used in the ornamentation of Chinese clothing, can be purchased at embroiderers' shops. But some ladies have quite a talent for inventing new patterns, and I have seen them working most beautiful original designs upon costly silks and satins, which it would be very difficult to find equalled in the shops where such articles are sold.

Chinese girls are betrothed at a very early age, sometimes as mere babies. Frequently a gentleman having a friend in a similar position in life with a little son, will promise, when the years of childhood are past, to give his daughter in marriage to the boy. A " mei-rin " or matchmaker will be employed, the children's horoscopes cast, and for several days the matter is under consideration of both families. If during this time of waiting any accident happens in either family, such as a breakage among the chinaware, or the loss of some trifling article, it is looked upon as an omen of evil, and the match is not concluded. But if all goes on quietly, the parents decide that the betrothal is a suitable one. A number of presents are then exchanged. Among them are two cards. One of these is ornamented with a gilt dragon, and has written upon it a number of particulars relating to the boy. The other is decorated with the picture of a phœnix, and gives similar information about the little girl. A thread of red silk with needles at either end is passed through each of these cards, which being exchanged, are preserved in the families of the children as signs of betrothal. In reference to this red silk, it is said that the feet of people destined to be married are tied together with invisible threads.

These engagements made by parents for their children are as binding as marriage, although the principal parties know nothing of the arrangements. Very sad surprises constantly occur at Chinese weddings, for frequently no communication takes place between the two families from the time of betrothal. Sometimes the family circumstances have greatly altered, and the father who has promised his child to the son of some wealthy man finds he has to give her up to a family in great poverty. Occasionally it is found that since the betrothal the bridegroom has become a helpless cripple. In another case of which I heard, the bride had been attacked by the terrible disease of leprosy ; and in another, the bridegroom had fallen a victim to that incurable malady.

When the
marriage day ar-
rives, the girl-
bride is brought
to her new home
in the grand
bridal chair of
brilliant scarlet,
elaborately de-
corated. None
of her friends
accompany her,
with the excep-
tion of two old
women, who act
the part which
is in England
allotted to the
girlish compan-
ions of the bride.
One of these old
women is the
go-between, or
match-maker,
and the other
takes the part of
mistress of the
ceremonies. The
bride's relatives
are supposed to
remain in their
own home and
bewail her loss.
When the door

THE BRIDAL CHAIR.

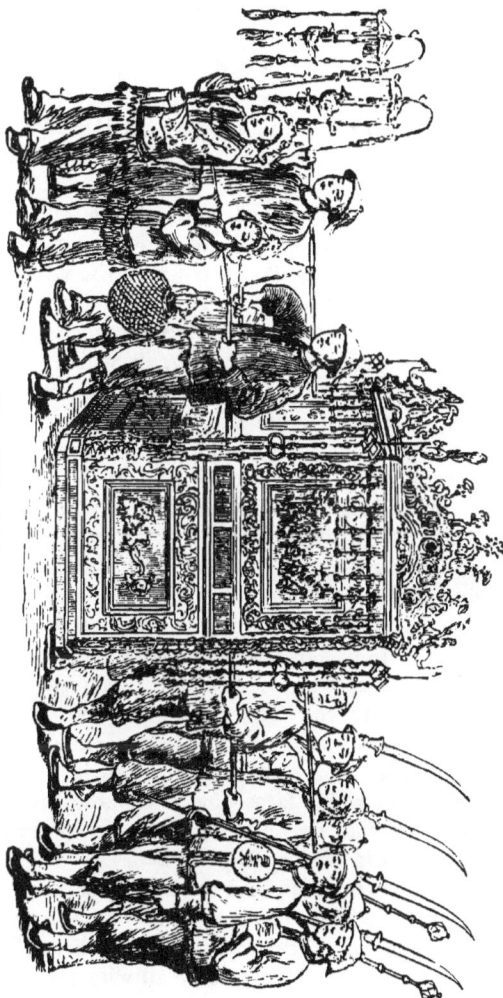

of the bridal chair is opened no flowing robes of white are revealed, for white is the colour of mourning, and must on no account be worn at a wedding. The little bride is usually attired in garments of various colours, but a large robe of scarlet is worn over all the rest. Her hair is adorned with a massive head-dress of gilt ornaments, and her head is covered with a veil of scarlet silk or cloth, which quite conceals her features.

At the wedding breakfast, at which the bride and bridegroom alone sit down, and of which the bride is never expected to partake, she sits motionless, her face still covered with the veil. They each drink out of two cups of wine, which are tied together with a silken thread. During this meal the mistress of ceremonies chants a song, supposed to be composed for the occasion, in which she predicts that every nuptial blessing shall be the portion of the young pair before her.

When the bridegroom has finished his repast, he leads his young wife into the decorated bridal chamber, where a large number of red boxes, containing the young lady's wardrobe, are piled up. The young husband then removes the veil, and for the first time looks upon the face of the girl who has become his wife. Soon after the bride and bridegroom together worship the spirit tablets of departed ancestors, and do reverence to the elder members of the family. A grand marriage feast is the climax of the day's festivities; and afterwards a large number of friends, both men and women, are admitted to look upon the face of the bride, and to make the most personal remarks upon her appearance. This is an ordeal through which every Chinese bride passes, and through a great part of the day I have frequently seen them standing, poor trembling girls, little more than children, with downcast, immovable faces—for a Chinese bride is taught that she must appear alike unconscious of blame or praise, of rude criticism or friendly words of sympathy.

The bride is not supposed to visit her parents till four months after the wedding. Not unfrequently this visit is a very sad one, when the young wife has to tell the story of some cruel and heartless mother-in-law, who makes life a torture to all who are in her power. Sad to say, these visits to the old home are often taken advantage of by miserable young wives to attempt to put an end to their lives. For life is so lightly valued by them that the taking of it seems only a very little thing.

But there are also comparatively happy marriages, considering the strange way in which they are brought about. Yet the life of all women in China is drearier or sadder than that of the men; and that must always be the case in lands where the compassionate teachings of the Christian religion are not known. For there might is right, and the weak ones have to suffer under the rule of the strong.

Should a girl in China lose her betrothed, or a young wife her husband, she is highly commended if she takes opium, or in some other way contrives to follow him into the unseen world. Outside the walls of many Chinese cities, as well as in some public streets, I have frequently seen monumental arches erected to perpetuate the memory of filial sons and daughters, or of young women who have killed themselves sooner than outlive their betrothed or their husband. Cases of this kind are reported to the Emperor, if the young lady is of a high social position, and these arches are erected at his command. A young lady connected with the family of a previous Chinese ambassador to England received this honour after death, and the case was reported in the pages of the *Pekin Gazette*, or official newspaper of China.

Many stories are related of the virtues possessed by heroines of past ages. Some of these are particularly warlike in spirit, but the leading idea in each is usually the cultivation of filial piety, and the devotion at all costs to a father's interests. I will give a condensed report of one of these stories, since they convey some idea of the virtues which are considered worthy of imitation by the daughters of the Flowery Land.

More than fourteen centuries ago there lived in the province of Hunan a celebrated general whose name was Wha. He had an only daughter who was called Moh-lan. This young lady had been duly instructed in all womanly arts, such as spinning, weaving, and embroidering; and in addition she had been taught to use the bow and arrow, and moreover was an accomplished horsewoman. General Wha was a brave commander, and his name was a terror to the border tribes which ravaged the empire. He was now, however, advanced in years, and had humbly petitioned the emperor for permission to retire from his laborious post. But the imperial army could ill afford to lose so noted a general, and the Son of Heaven insisted that the aged and feeble soldier should, under pain of his heaviest displeasure, take up his position at 'the head of the troops. The imperial couriers delivered their message to the sick commander, and Moh-lan, sitting at her loom behind the curtains of the apartments of the women, heard the order also, and knew that it must be obeyed. She had no brother to take his father's place and lead the troops to victory. She was only a girl, but she rose to the occasion, and determined to do all that a son might have done. The decision was no sooner made than carried out. Hastily she encased her small feet in her father's military boots, then seizing his weapons, with his plumed hat upon her head, she sprung upon his noble war-horse, and galloped away to put herself at the head of the army. Seeing the familiar arms and trappings of their beloved commander, the troops supposed the maiden to be some young officer who had been appointed at his request to lead them, and gladly followed to victory. For more than ten years after this Moh-lan's course was one of uninterrupted success. At last every enemy was subdued, and the land was at peace. Only then did Moh-lan return to her old home, to find that her venerated father had passed away, and her other relatives were doubtful of her identity. At length they were convinced, and received her with open arms. The Emperor, when he heard it rumoured that his all-conquering commander was but a woman, sent for her to court, and gave her hand in marriage to one of the high officers of state. When she died a splendid monument was erected by imperial command to commemorate her filial piety and patriotism.

CHAPTER VII.

IT was in the year 1858 that the second war between Great Britain and China was commenced. Before its close in 1860 the allied armies had laid in smoking ruins the walls of the beautiful Summer Palace near Peking, the grand home of the Chinese emperors.

Great was the commotion at the capital when the tidings arrived that the foreign soldiers were really on their way to the imperial city.

The news was brought to Peking by swift couriers, and carried on from thence to the Emperor's residence.

Guards, who had been placed along the road at short intervals within hearing of each other, passed the alarming news from lip to lip till it reached the palace in a wonderfully short space of time.

It was immediately decided that the court should at once take its departure for a country residence of the Emperor, distant about eight days' journey, and called by the name of Yeh-ho, or Warm Streams.

There was no time for preparation, the whole city was in confusion, and it was a motley throng of strangely-attired attendants which followed in the Emperor's train as he commenced his flight. It was a weary journey they had to make, fording streams and travelling over rough and uneven ground.

Even the Emperor had to endure many hardships, for, in the alarm and confusion of starting, no preparations had been made for the journey.

Every one was rejoiced when the grand gates of the palace of Yeh-ho came in sight. Situated in the midst of fine pleasure-grounds adorned with firs and cypress, and many other trees, under whose shade herds of deer and elk roamed unmolested, it was a beautiful place of refuge; and yet the Emperor Hien-Feng had only been induced by urgent necessity to take up his abode there. People said it was an unlucky residence for any of his race, for his grandfather, the Emperor Chia-Ching, had died there.

After some time of suspense news came to Yeh-ho that the court might safely return to Peking. But the reports of the doings of the "foreign barbarians" filled their hearts with fear, and the Emperor decided to remain over the winter in his quiet retreat. He never saw the ruins of his fair Summer Palace, for he died at Yeh-ho before the spring.

When he "ascended the Dragon Throne above," or was "received as a guest on high" (which is the way in which the Chinese speak of the death of their ruler), he left behind him a little son, who was at the time only six years of age. This little boy had been placed under the guardianship of the two empresses, who were both the wives of his father. One was called the Empress of the East, and she was the greatest lady; the other was the child's own mother, and she was called the Western Empress. Chinese emperors are not known by their own name, it would be thought disrespectful to have that in common use, so a title or reign name is selected for them when they come to the throne. This little boy was proclaimed emperor under a name which means "Fortunate Union."

It was soon discovered that many of the great men of the empire were plotting to get rid of the guardians of the little boy, and take the management of affairs into their own hands.

This conspiracy was discovered by the Empresses, who, with the young Emperor under their care, left Yeh-ho and came to Peking. A clever man, named Prince Kung, who was also one of those who had charge of the little Emperor, had a number of these plotters put to death. On account of this affair the reign name was changed, and it was afterwards known as Tung-chi, which means "United Rule."

The two imperial ladies who had charge of the little boy are said to be very wise and clever women. This is, no doubt, true, or they would not have kept for so long the reins of government in their hands.

Some time ago, it is said, a high mandarin tried to make mischief between the two ladies. He used to fabricate complaints, which he said each had made against the other. The two Empresses compared notes, and so discovered the designs of the courtier, and they immediately ordered him to swallow gold-leaf, which was only a way of commanding him to pay the penalty of his life for his foolish conduct.

In the year 1872 Tung-chi, who was then a boy of sixteen, was married. Before the new Empress had been publicly announced, a large number of girls from all the principal families in the empire were ordered to be sent up to the palace, that the Empresses might make a selection from among them.

PRINCE KUNG.

Rumour said that some time before the Imperial ladies had decided upon the girl who was to be raised to this honour. Her name was Aluteh, and she was the daughter of a member of the Imperial College, known as Duke Chung.

The gossips of Peking said that the friends of Aluteh would gladly have guarded her against the perilous honour which they feared might await her, for she was a girl of singular beauty and intelligence. It was said that so determined were they to do all in their power to prevent the choice falling upon her that they placed rolls of wadding about her shoulders, beneath her dress, to give her the appearance of being deformed.

But the Empresses were too clever for the anxious parents, for, having fixed upon her as the bride, they issued a notification to the effect that although the youthful Empress had been deformed, the court physician had been able, with much skill, to remove the protuberances from her back, and she was now so straight and graceful that it was evidently the will of Heaven that she should be promoted to the high position of Empress.

The young lady who was thus exalted had little of happiness in her short life, though much grandeur attended the wedding ceremonies. On the day before the marriage, three princes were appointed by the young Emperor to go and burn incense, offering sacrifices at the temple, and informing Heaven of the important event about to take place. Two other princes were also deputed to go on similar errands. One had to convey the news to Mother Earth, and the other to pay a visit to the temple of the Emperor's ancestors, carrying the news to them. Less than two years after the wedding, it was announced that the young Emperor had " met with the joy of having the small-pox," for that disease, though very prevalent in China, is looked upon as a mark of Heaven's special favour.

A few days after, the news of his sickness was succeeded by tidings of the Emperor's death, and his young wife was shortly after reported to have died of grief. Some said, however, that the Dowager Empresses had commanded her to put an end to her life at once, and that she had starved herself in obedience to their order.

It was necessary immediately to select a new Emperor, and, according to Chinese ideas, he could not be of an older generation than the young Tung-chi, though several of his uncles were still living. For the peace of the Empire the dead ruler's spirit must be regularly worshipped and have sacrifices offered to it, and this could only be done by one of the same generation as himself.

The council of the imperial family met at night within one of the palace chambers, and they decided that a little boy, about three and a half years of age, should be chosen Emperor. The child was the son of Prince Chung, the seventh son of the Emperor Tau-Kwang, and the brother of Hien-Feng.

The little Emperor was sent for immediately, tired and sleepy as he was, and placed in the midst of his uncles, who all did homage to him. The first consequence of the act by which the baby-boy Tsai-tien was changed into the Emperor Kwang-Su, or "Illustrious Successor," was the retirement of his father from public life, since, according to Chinese ideas, it was quite impossible for a father to do homage to his own son. But even this matter had to be arranged in what seems to Europeans a very round-about way.

The Emperor's father sent up a memorial to the two Dowager Empresses—for these ladies now undertook the care of Kwang-Su, as they had previously done of his predecessor.

Prince Chung described the agony of grief into which he was thrown when called upon to gaze upon the features of the departed Emperor. But he was even more overwhelmed by the news that his own son had been chosen to succeed to the throne. He was carried home as one bereft of reason, he was attacked by many diseases, and begged to be allowed to spend the remnant of his miserable life in the seclusion of his own home, entreating the Empresses to withdraw his double allowance as an Imperial Prince.

This memorial, which reads so strangely to English ears, seemed quite correct and proper to the educated Chinese, and appeared in the pages of the court newspaper.

References to the little Emperor's education and training may often be found in the pages of the *Pekin Gazette*, and are also frequently floating about like the common rumours of other courts. Kwang-Su is described as a delicate little lad, thin and pale, which is not to be wondered at, since it is said he is often called up in the middle of

the night when State business is in progress, so as to be trained to
official etiquette and the management of affairs of State.

Poor little fellow! doubtless he sometimes wishes he were not an
Emperor at all, but could sleep at night like other boys.

In one matter perhaps some English boys may think he is rather
fortunate. Some time ago, in the pages of the *Pekin Gazette*, the
appointment of a "whipping boy" was announced—that is, a little
fellow whose duty it was to receive all the punishments which might
be deserved by the little Emperor when he committed a fault. He
stood, indeed, in the same relation to Kwang-Su as we are informed by the author of *Waverley* Sir Mungo Malagrowther did to the
son of Mary Queen of Scots. In the same paper there may sometimes
be found mention of some curious presents which have been received
by the child-ruler. Not long since there was the following announcement:— "The horse which was presented to Us by Poyennamoku
was quiet and steady when We rode it. Let it, therefore, be called
'The Pearl that flies like a bird.'" From a place far off in Mongolia
they send the little Emperor every year two cases of jam, of which I
suppose he is very fond, since a few years ago the people sent
many apologies because the season had been so cold that the
fruit would not ripen, and consequently there was no jam to be had.

Poor little Chinese Emperor! shut up in his grand palace, taught
always to behave with the greatest propriety and to act with
great gravity, according to the rules of court etiquette—most English
boys and girls, however humble their homes and surroundings, are
doubtless much happier than he.

CHAPTER VIII.

RAT-TAT-TAT! Bang—bang! On all sides there were such strange noises that one might have imagined a volley of artillery was being exploded. These were the sounds that awoke me at the hour of midnight when I had been for only two days a dweller in the Celestial Empire. What could be the matter? Were the inhabitants of the far-famed mart of Hankow turning out *en masse* to hold the fort against some attacking enemy?

It was nothing very serious after all, for I soon found that the cannonading which was deafening my ears was nothing more than the continuous letting off of fireworks to frighten away the spirits of evil which it was feared might be prowling around on New Year's morning.

It was the dawn of the greatest festival of the Chinese year, and the people had for days past been making the most extensive preparations to celebrate it. It had been a time of general house-cleaning everywhere. New charms and scrolls had been bought to decorate and protect each home. New clothes had been purchased or taken out of pawn, and nearly everybody looked smiling and good-tempered, since the great holiday and rest of the year was at hand.

There is no weekly day of rest in China, the shops are open and the streets full of eager buyers and sellers every day alike. When the missionaries go through the streets to the Christian chapels on the Sabbath-day, they are often saddened as they pass through the midst of these busy crowds. The multitudes of those who are bowing down to gods of wood and stone are so great, they seem for a time to blot out the encouraging thought of the "little flock" which is being gathered out of the midst of these Chinese cities—men and women, and even little children, who have heard the glad tidings of Jesus' love, and are trying to follow in His footsteps.

A month in China commences with a new moon, and so New Year's Day is not on the first of January, as with us, but very frequently quite at the end of our first month, or even as late as the second or third week of February.

Very few Chinamen ever think of retiring to rest on New Year's Eve. They have an idea that watching for the dawn of New Year's morning several years in succession will ensure to them long life. Even the children of Chinese families usually sit up, as we say, to see the New Year in, but they call it "to round the year." In some parts a few faggots of pine wood are lighted in a space before the stand upon which the ancestral tablets are placed. The boys and girls greatly enjoy the fun of exploding crackers and throwing handfuls of salt upon the flames. The crackling sound made by the burning salt is thought to be an omen of good.

Santa Claus is not known to Chinese juveniles, but late on New Year's Eve it is common for the head of a family to present the children and servants of the household with some copper cash strung on a scarlet cord, since it is considered unlucky to begin the year with an empty purse.

The last night of the old year is always a busy time with tradespeople in China, for every one is expected to pay their debts contracted during the year. If it is not possible to discharge them in full, they must at any rate pay off a considerable portion of them before the new year dawns. When once the great day arrives, nothing but peace and goodwill is supposed to reign, and if a man is still in debt, his creditor is not expected to press his claim again till some months at least have passed.

As all shops will be closed for several days, it is necessary that every family should lay in a good stock of provisions. It used to be the custom for most shops to be closed for a fortnight; and the lovers of old customs often bemoan the fact that year after year shops are being opened earlier, and the necessaries of life can be readily bought when the year is four or five days old. The longer a tradesman keeps his shop closed the more respectable he is considered by his neighbours.

The first ceremony which a Chinaman performs when the hour of midnight has passed and the new year has been entered, is to worship before the spirit tablets of his ancestors and at the shrine of the household gods. After this the whole family go out of the front door of the house, while the women and servants of the household lift up lamps or torches to give them light. They then bow down and do reverence towards a part of the heavens which has been indicated in the almanac. This is commonly spoken of as the worship of heaven and earth, though it is described in the almanac as the ceremony of receiving the spirit of gladness or good fortune, which it has been ascertained will come out of that quarter of the heavens.

This is considered by a Chinaman the most important moment of the year. He has a terrible dread lest his "first foot," as they say in Scotland, should be a person who will bring him ill-fortune—a shaven priest, for instance. The first words he hears too have a fearful significance to him, should they unfortunately refer to fire, shipwreck, loss of office, failure in business, an evil spirit, a serpent, sickness, separation or death. And not only the words themselves significant of these things are unlucky, but other words with quite a different meaning but a similar sound to the unfortunate phrases. On the other hand, if some words relating to prosperity and gladness are the first that greet his ear, the Chinaman's heart is filled with joy, and he thinks he may reasonably anticipate a Happy New Year. Going out into the streets in the early morning of this great holiday, we should find them strewn with the crimson paper of exploded crackers. These fireworks are believed to be very effectual in driving away evil spirits. It is said that the original idea in their manufacture was to imitate the crackling sound of burning bamboos, which were once used for the same purpose. Beggars always throng the streets at this time, and reap a large harvest, since no one cares to refuse to give them a trifle, lest they should have to begin the year with a curse, even if it be only from a beggar's lips. Many rich men give very liberally at this great festival; tickets for rice are widely distributed, and sums of money, frequently given anonymously, are sent to the families of the very poor.

The front doors of most of the houses are usually decorated with new "mên shin," or door spirits, on New Year's morning. These are gaudily-coloured pictures of two generals of past ages. It is said that the Emperor who was at that time reigning in China had a dream, in which he was informed that evil spirits were attempting to invade his palace. To prevent their entrance, he commanded two of his bravest warriors to keep guard at the palace gates. The spirits, frightened by their warlike appearance, were afraid to enter, and since the death of these famous generals, it is said their pictures have been found to

A STREET BEGGAR.

be equally efficacious. These pictures remain upon the doors all through the year, though the beating of the wind and rain upon them often leaves little but dilapidated fragments when the last month comes.

Above the doors a bunch of cypress, together with some sheets of mock money and gold and silver paper ingots, is hung, and doorways are often decorated with fringes of scarlet paper fancifully cut out, having fastened upon it the character which stands for happiness. Strips of scarlet paper as scrolls are also used to decorate the interior of the houses, the motto written upon them having always some fortunate meaning.

On New Year's morning, when a Chinaman meets a friend, he clasps his own hands, and moving them up and down before him, encased in his long sleeves, bows low and repeats the words, " kung-she, kung-she," or, " I congratulate you," which is equivalent to our phrase, " I wish you a happy New Year."

Many people do not make ceremonious calls on New Year's Day, but defer them till a day or two later. Not a few, wearied out with the vigil and ceremonies of the night, spend the day in rest and quiet. Only here and there you hear the sounds that seem to be so musical to Chinese ears—the banging of gongs or cymbals, or the squeaking of a Chinese flute. Every one who is abroad is dressed in their best clothing ; the children are perfectly gorgeous in their coats of many colours, while the shoes, caps, and collars of the babies are all decorated with many-coloured embroidery. As the weather is cold, all the garments are wadded, and the children look like so many round balls, or, when a little older, something like bolsters. We begin to wonder sometimes where all the grand apparel has been kept all the year ; and at this season foreigners are not unfrequently puzzled by the arrival, among other visitors, of a gentleman who, to a new-comer, would doubtless appear to be moving in a high position in society. There is probably something familiar about the features of the visitor who thus calls to offer his congratulations. The mystery is explained when the foreigner is informed that the gorgeously-attired gentleman is Mr. So-and-So's cook, or some workman whom he has employed during the year.

Feasting, visiting, gambling, and seeing theatrical performances are some of the amusements of the season. Nearly every evening fireworks are let off in great quantities. On the fourth day of the month preparations are made for receiving back again the god of the kitchen, who, it is supposed, has been absent, spending his New Year's holidays in the invisible regions, since the twenty-fourth of the twelfth month. He is believed to have carried thither a report of the conduct of the family during the past year. A paper horse and various other things necessary for his journey are usually burned by the household on the evening of his supposed departure. Throughout the whole of the New Year's festivities, idolatrous worship, either of spirits or of gods, is so intermixed with social customs as to make that season a very trying one to Chinese Christians. They are always unmercifully persecuted by their heathen friends when they refuse to take part in idolatrous ceremonies. One boy I knew was so convinced that it was wrong to worship the false gods, or to bow before the ancestral tablets, that he begged his father to excuse him from it. When the man knew his son had been hearing of the true God in the Glad Tidings Hall of the neighbouring city, his anger knew no bounds. He stripped the boy of all his outer clothing, and after giving him a severe beating, sent him out into the streets.

Not unfrequently at this season some of the gods are taken out for a ride in sedan chairs. It is believed that the families residing in the streets along which they pass will be free from sickness and pestilence during the year.

The fifteenth of the first moon brings with it the great Feast of Lanterns, when the city is illuminated with lanterns suspended on long poles from the roofs of the houses. The scene seems changed into a city of fairy-land, for even the poorest families put out a lantern above the roof of their cottage. They do not burn long, and one after another the lights die out, but the revelry in the houses and the frequent explosion of fireworks continue till far on into the night. On the evening of the Feast of Lanterns more women are seen upon the streets than at other times, custom allowing them to come out and witness the grand illumination.

I have spoken first of the New Year's festivals, since they are by far the most important. There is another, however, which often precedes it, according to our reckoning of time, while in the Chinese calendar it is often oddly arranged that the festival of "Welcoming the Spring" occurs in the last month of the year. The great feature in the procession which is formed in honour of the day is a life-size figure of a water buffalo—the common domestic animal of China. The framework is composed of bamboo splints, covered with paper of various colours. The sheets are said to be pasted on either by a blind man or under the direction of a fortune-teller, and are believed to predict the weather of the year, and also to give curious information on various other subjects. If there is much white paper, rains and floods are expected to prevail over the land ; if red predominates, there will be many fires, and the summer will prove unusually hot. Yellow indicates plentiful harvests, and a favourable year is thus predicted.

The ceremony of "receiving the spring" takes place outside the east gate of the city, since it is from the East that spring is supposed to come. An altar is usually erected before the figure of the buffalo, and the god of the land and grain ; then the prefect of the city, with other mandarins, attired in their richest robes, do reverence before them. The same evening, the paper buffalo is broken up into fragments, and the man who succeeds in obtaining a portion of it fancies that in consequence his own buffalo will prosper during the year.

The next great festival occurs in the bright spring-tide of the year, when the country is fragrant with the sweet scent of the bean-flower, and the willows and graceful bamboos are looking lovely in their fresh foliage. Schoolboys at this time receive a few days' vacation, in order that they may take part in this festival, which, like all Chinese holidays, has a religious signification. It is known as Tsing-Ming, and is the festival of the tombs. At this time every Chinaman visits the graves of his ancestors, burning incense and paper money, and offering sacrifices there. So universal is this custom that if these ceremonies are neglected for three years in succession, or, at any rate, if for that period the sheets of paper-money, kept in place by stones or a heap of earth, are not seen upon the graves, the land is liable to be taken possession of by its original owners, and the plot sold to another family. Chinese burying-grounds are always outside the walls of their cities. It is an impressive sight to see the innumerable mounds of earth, many of them unmarked by tree or stone, others with a small slab at the head bearing the name and date of death of the departed. The tombs of the wealthier families are usually on some hill-side, on a spot specially chosen by geomancers, but I am speaking of the graves of the common people. They stretch away over the grassy plains farther than the eye can reach, till it sometimes seems as if the cities of the dead in China were even more densely crowded than the cities of the living.

A day is always fixed in the Imperial Calendar for the commencement of this festival, which is sometimes spoken of as the Sweeping of the Graves, but the actual visit to the tombs can be made either a few days before or after, to suit the convenience of the families. Before the ceremonies commence, some members of the family put in order the little plot of ground, pulling up the weeds and tall rank grass which have grown wild above it. Whole families come out and take part in the service—women and children as well as men. They carry with them little basins containing various kinds of food, such as fish and fowl, pork, and cakes of different kinds. These, with cups of wine, are ranged in order before the grave, and candles and incense having been lighted, one by one the men and boys of the family, according to age, stand up, reverently bowing and knocking their heads to the ground. After this a large quantity of paper-money is burnt to supply the spirits with pocket-money for their various needs, and then a number of crackers are exploded. Offerings are then made to the god who is supposed to be in charge of that part of the country, and food is also arranged at a little distance from the graves, and offered to the beggar spirits, which are supposed to be as numerous in the spirit-world as in the streets of Chinese cities. Whenever departed spirits receive a large offering from their descendants, it is considered certain that the beggar-spirits will behave as they would do in this world, and so by their demands for charity disturb the relatives of the worshippers, and prevent them from enjoying their feast in peace. Therefore the beggars receive an offering as well as the friends, and in this way it is believed all are satisfied.

Standing by one of these graves one day at this festival, on a bright spring evening, I saw a family going through these ceremonies, and a very little boy was with them. He watched his elders carefully, and then was put up to clasp his small hands and do reverence also. When the worship was over we began to talk to the little company. "Why do you let a child so small take part in this service?" we asked, looking at the little fellow, who seemed greatly to enjoy the burning of the paper and exploding of the crackers. The father, a grave, courteous Chinaman, replied, "We bring them thus early to teach them their duty, so that when they grow older they may never neglect to worship at the tombs, and will attend to our wants when we have passed into the spirit-world."

Upon returning home the people carry with them small branches of trees, slips of firs, or boughs of wild azaleas. These sprays of greenery are usually placed in a vase before the spirit tablets in the home of the family. To some of the poor people living in the towns this is their only day in the country during the year.

Over the doors of the houses, during the time of this festival, a willow-branch is usually suspended. It is believed to be useful in attracting the spirits of the dead to come and partake of the essence of food prepared for them and placed before the ancestral tablets as well as at the graves. It is also believed that not only the spirits of the dead but a large number of evil spirits are set free to visit the earth at this feast, and the willow-branch, while it attracts the spirits related to the family, frightens away any that are not welcome.

II

The festival which ranks next, in a Chinese boy's estimation, to the grand New Year's holiday, is the Feast of the Dragon Boats. It is sometimes spoken of as the "Children's Festival." The great feature in the festivities is the racing of the dragon boats, of which, in populous cities, there are sometimes twenty or more. These boats are long and narrow, and will carry from ten to thirty men. The body and stern are gaily painted, and the bow is shaped like the raised head of a dragon with gaping jaws. A large drum is placed in the centre of the boat, and much noise is made by beating gongs. A boy sitting up on the dragon's head directs the movements of the rowers with a flag which he holds in his hands.

Crowds of people assemble on the river banks to watch the boats and the racing. The successful crews receive prizes, and much jealousy is excited, and quarrels and fights often conclude the day's performances. Accidents not unfrequently occur from the boats coming into collision with each other.

This grand Chinese holiday had its origin in an event which occurred about 500 B.C. At that time there lived a very wise and prudent minister of state, whose name was Ken Yuen. The prince he served was a man of violent temper and bad character, and when petitioned by his minister to introduce some reforms into the government of the country, he degraded and at last dismissed him. Unable to survive the disgrace he had sustained, Ken Yuen flung himself into the river, and thus put an end to his life. Some fishermen who saw him disappear searched diligently for his body, but it was not found. Ever since, upon the anniversary of the death of this honest official, boats have gone out casting offerings on the river for the spirit of the departed, and going through the ceremony of searching for his body.

On one occasion, it is said, the holiday-making worshippers were surprised by the appearance of Ken Yuen himself, who complained that the offerings intended for him were always stolen by an enormous reptile that made its home in the waters. Since that time the dragon boats have been used at this festival, with the idea of frightening away the reptile of which Ken Yuen complained.

In the eighth month of the year the Festival of the Moon is held ; it is sometimes called the " Feast of Rewarding the Moon."

Chinese children do not talk of the " Man in the Moon," but they say there is a rabbit there engaged in pounding rice, or, some say, medicines.

At this feast everybody eats moon-cakes, which can be obtained in great variety. Most of them are round like the moon, but they have curious figures on them, such as fishes and animals, among them the mythical rabbit. Some are painted with spots of bright colour, and others adorned with gold-leaf.

The worship of the Moon is one of great antiquity in all nations. The prophet Jeremiah refers to the worship of the Queen of Heaven in his day, and to the incense that was burned and the cakes that were offered before her.

The Chinese say that their festival has an historical origin. The story they tell is as follows :—One evening, the Emperor Ming Wong was walking in his palace grounds accompanied by some of his priestly advisers. The conversation turned upon the question, " Was the Moon inhabited or not ? " The tutor of the young prince replied by asking him if he would like to pay a visit to it and see. He answered in the affirmative. The priest then threw his staff into the air, and it became a bridge over which he and his pupil passed to the brilliant luminary. They found it inhabited by beautiful women, who lived in magnificent palaces surrounded by charming gardens. The prince would fain have lingered amid these scenes of loveliness, but was called upon by his tutor to depart. On their way to earth the priest asked his pupil to play upon his lute, which he carried with him, and of which he was very fond. They were just drawing near to the city of Nanking, and hearing what they concluded was celestial music, the inhabitants rushed to the roofs of their houses. The prince, advised by his companion, showered down upon the people the cash he carried with him.

Upon his return to his palace the prince was inclined to fancy all his adventures had been undertaken in the land of dreams, when a

G 2/4619

memorial was received from the Governor-general of the province over which he had passed, telling a story of wonderful music and showers of cash which had been heard and seen by the inhabitants of that district on the fifteenth of the eighth month.

Of course the Emperor was convinced that his trip to the Moon was a reality, and ordered that henceforth the people should set apart the day on which he made his wonderful journey as a time of general rejoicing—a festival in honour of the Moon.

NEW YEAR'S MODE OF SALUTATION.

CHAPTER IX.

CHINESE IDOLATRY AND SUPERSTITIONS.

" How do Chinese children learn to worship idols ? " I can imagine you asking.

Come with me and I will take you to one of their great gloomy temples.

Not on a Sabbath, for there is no day of rest in China, but either on the first or fifteenth of the month, for these are the dates upon which people usually visit the temples.

We must go up the flight of wide stone steps at the entrance, and as we enter shall see two tall images with very ugly faces and brilliantly painted coats, which are called " Guardians of the Gate."

Walking on into the temple, which looks dull and shadowy in the dim light, we shall come to the shrine of the great idol in whose honour the temple was built. A number of other images are ranged around it : they are the servants of the god, and large rings of incense are burning before it.

In some temples Buddhist priests sit in rows repeating in a sort of chant words of prayer which they do not understand at all, since they are in another language. See the mothers bringing their little children forward and teaching them to clasp their hands and bow down, knocking their heads to the ground as they worship the senseless idol ! If it is the first time, the children are afraid, and sometimes say, " I can't do it. I never shall do it." Then they watch closely while their mothers once more show them how it is done. Afterwards they are sometimes rewarded with little presents, which they are told have been given to them by the idol. But if they are terrified and afraid to worship, they are told stories of the terrible things that happen to people who do not ask the protection of the ugly idols.

Nearly all the gods in whose honour Chinese temples are erected are the images of people who lived in India or China hundreds or thousands of years ago, and have since been deified and are worshipped. It is the same as if in England people were to bow down before images of King Alfred, Shakespeare, Lord Nelson, or the Duke of Wellington.

Sometimes, soon after children have been worshipping at a temple, they will fall ill, or some accident will happen to them. Then the parents immediately fancy the child has offended the god, and do all they can to make it forget its anger.

One night, when we were coming home from our week-night service in the city of Wuchang, we passed a temple brightly lighted up. It had been built in honour of the god of the land and grain. It is unusual to see people worshipping at a temple late in the evening, and we turned aside to look at the people bending there. Two men were very devoutly burning incense and paper money, and their faces were very sad. When they had finished and were preparing to leave, we asked why they had come to the temple at so late an hour. The elder of the two men turned towards us a very anxious face and replied, "It is just three days now since I with my only son came here to worship. On the way home my little boy had a serious fall, which has injured him severely. He is now very ill, and I fear may not recover. I feel sure he must in some way have offended the god, and so I have brought large quantities of paper money and am sacrificing at this shrine, hoping that his anger may be turned away, and then my child will recover."

How thankful we were to be able to do something to comfort the poor idol worshipper! We told him of a Father in heaven who loves all His children, and who alone could make the little boy well again.

Let me take you to one or two more of the many temples in this city in which I have been living. Quite near to the Mission House is one in connection with a large printing establishment. It contains an immense gilt figure of Buddha, who, they say, leads people to the western heaven. Before this enormous figure you may often see offerings of flowers and rice placed. A large number of Buddhist priests live in the monastery adjoining this temple. They dress in long loose yellow robes, and their heads, being shaven, are quite bald. They may not eat meat, but live solely upon vegetables and rice. The gong is sounding for their mid-day meal. The abbot sits on a daïs in the centre of the refectory, and the priests are ranged in rows on either side of him. There are about sixty monks living in this place. Before they take their meal they sing or chant a grace, but they do not understand the words they sing. A little of the food is then placed as an offering on a stone slab just outside the door. They eat their meal in perfect silence. When all have finished, and the chopsticks are placed in order by the side of the blue basins, the gong is again struck, and the priests file out silently one by one.

Buddhists think it is an act of very great merit to preserve the life of any animal, and frequently when people come to worship at these temples they make a vow that they will preserve the life of some living creature. So one frequently sees in Buddhist temples, fowls, ducks, and geese, or pigs and sheep, and also a pond filled with fish which have been rescued from the tanks in which they are exposed for sale by the fishmongers. At one temple I once saw a very ancient pig. The priests said it was a hundred years old, which was of course untrue. But it must have been quite venerable for a pig, and was such a deplorable-looking object that the next time I was there, I was not sorry to hear that the pig was dead. Some people make a vow to release a large number of sparrows. These birds are kept—a large number together—in cages hanging outside the poulterers' shops; people buy twenty or thirty of them for the purpose of setting them free.

Just outside the east gate of the city of Wuchang there is a celebrated temple known as the Temple of Hades, and the god who is

BUDDHIST PRIESTS.

supposed to rule in the unseen regions is worshipped there. The first figure that would attract your notice is one far above life-size, with a black beard, and flowing white robes, wearing a tall conical hat, with an umbrella over his shoulder. In his hand he holds the end of a chain, which is fastened round the representation of the wasted form of a dying man, and he is supposed to be dragging him along to judgment. When you ask a Chinaman what he thinks will happen to him when he dies, a common answer is, "Oh, Wutsang will come for me, I suppose."

The little burial-ground belonging to the Chinese Christians is just outside the grim walls of this temple. Sometimes when we have gathered round the grave side, to hold a short service before committing to the earth the remains of some departed Christian, crowds from the heathen temple have come and joined us. How strange the glad words of triumphant faith sounded to them! they know nothing of a bright hope beyond the grave, a rest "prepared for the people of God."

At both sides of this temple of Hades are some terrible groups of figures which are too frightful for me to describe to you in detail. I only mention them at all that you may see how sad and hopeless is the heathen faith from which we are seeking to win these people. These groups represent persons being judged for their sins, and some are enduring the punishments of the Buddhist hell. Here you see the figure of a man standing before the judges of the unseen world. He is on a raised platform, and a mirror is hung before him in which he will see reflected the form he is to assume when born into the world again. The man is starting back in horror as he sees the figure of an ox reflected there.

But before this second birth, they believe he has to endure many fearful tortures, and in successive groups we see him surrounded by demons who are engaged in tormenting him. He is thrown on a hill of knives, sawn asunder, tied to a pillar heated red hot, boiled in oil, and pounded in a mortar. Before he is born into the world again he must drink of the tea of forgetfulness, which is represented as being sold by two old women who sit at the gates of Hades. This tea, they say, makes men lose all remembrance of their former lives on earth.

At the feet of the tall image with the chain there are always heaps of shoes lying—offerings from people who believe the idol has listened to their entreaties and spared the lives of their friends: Here is a baby-boy's tiny slipper, and there the shoe of a grown-up man.

Oh, how sad it makes one to go into these places and see people trusting in these useless idols! Sometimes I have seen men kneeling before these shrines pleading very earnestly. One, I remember, was asking that his life might long be spared; and another, who was troubled with asthma, prayed that when the time came for Wutsang to drag him away he would remember how short his breath was, and walk slowly.

Another famous temple is the Yellow Stork Tower, a low pagoda, to which the following story is attached :—Long, long ago there lived in this city of Wuchang a man named Shin, who was in

THE YELLOW STORK TOWER.

business as a wine merchant. Now it happened that among the occasional frequenters of this house was a man whose name was Lu-Tsou. To this customer Mr. Shin had always shown much kindness, treating him as an intimate friend, and never being at all particular about the payment of the wine account. The thought had never entered the wine merchant's head that the person he was

WUCHANG.

treating so hospitably was other than an ordinary mortal, till one day, Lu-Tsou, as a token of gratitude for the kindness he had received, turned the water of a well in Mr. Shin's garden into wine. At the same time he took an orange, and dividing it into four quarters, murmured over it some potent charm, and immediately it was changed into a stork, and settled upon a high pole in the wine merchant's garden. The fame of the wonderful stork and the delicately flavoured wine spread through the city, and customers thronged Mr. Shin's house till he became so wealthy that, in gratitude to his benefactor, he determined to build in his honour a fine temple, or three-storied pagoda. It stands there to-day, and from its upper story a fine view is obtained of the surrounding country. The broad stream of the magnificent Yang-tse-kiang flows past it. On the farther shore are the craggy slopes of the Hanyang hill, crowned with its white-walled temple, while the thickly populated mart of Hankow stretches away at its foot. From the opposite side of the tower we look out upon the grand provincial city, which is cut into three portions by low green hills, while the dwellings of the city lie crowded together in the valleys. Here and there the scene is relieved by the queer curled caves of some temples or guilds, or the walled gardens of some official's residence.

This Yellow Stork Tower, with the temples rising up one behind another in its rear, form the principal recreation ground of the city. The lower story of the tower is always thronged with fortune-tellers and gambling tables.

A Tauist priest stands at the foot of the winding staircase and begs a few cash of each visitor. Crowds of Chinamen are usually sitting round little tables in the upper story, enjoying a cup of tea with cakes and melon seeds, for the wine and the wonderful well of the legend have disappeared. In the centre of the top story there is an image of the deified philosopher Lu-Tsou, playing on his lute, while he sits on the back of a stork, which with outspread wings is preparing to carry him through the regions of space. But the strangest sight of all is to be found in one of the temples behind the tower. This is the image of a god fast asleep, kept under a glass case! When Lu-Tsou goes through that part of the country, they say he stops and sleeps there. Are you not reminded of a text in your Bibles which tells us of the unceasing care of God over His people, and says "Behold He that keepeth Israel shall neither slumber nor sleep"?

There are many more temples, hundreds I could tell you of in most great Chinese cities.

I have told you something of one or two, but should like to mention one more situated in a lovely spot, not in Wuchang, but on the Orphan Island, in the Poyang Lake.

Let me tell you of a visit I paid to it once. We had been on a journey of many days in our little boat on that great lake, and in returning, anchored our small craft at the foot of the flight of steps, and climbed up the steep ascent till we reached the temple buildings. The whole island was like a garden, the grey old rocks being covered with lovely climbing plants, while the fragrance of the Chinese jessamine scented the air. Inside the temple were a multitude of gods of various names, but the one that interested me more than any other was the shrine of the Goddess of Mercy. There she sat on a throne decorated with magnificent carving, and over her head was a canopy composed of cloth of gold. But what attracted me most was two large screens on either side of the apartment, which were completely covered from top to bottom with offerings in the shape of beautiful embroidered leaves or tiny banners, which had each been worked by some woman or girl in the neighbourhood. Some came from homes of grinding poverty, where every cash was needed to purchase daily food. And yet every one seemed to have used the finest and best materials, no one grudged denying themselves in order to present this offering to the useless idol which had no power to help or save. As I looked at the beautiful work and thought of the skilful fingers which had embroidered this miniature landscape, of the girlish hands which had traced this simple border of flowers, how I longed for the time when the glad news of Jesus, all powerful to save, shall brighten every Chinese home! Do we always offer to the Saviour who died for us the best we have to give, anything that costs no self-denial and is

ORPHAN ISLAND, POYANG LAKE.

a real sacrifice to us—or are the heathen more in earnest than we are ?

If I were to go on to tell you the names only of all the gods and goddesses worshipped in China, you would grow quite tired of hearing them, there are so many. So I will only mention a few of the principal ones.

A very strange thing about them is that the greater number of the people whose images are now worshipped as gods in China, are by no means individuals whom we should feel inclined to reverence or even respect, if we are to believe the stories told of them by their worshippers.

There is a God of Thieves, who is said to have been a great thief himself in former days ; another god to which gamblers go for help ; and even a god of swine, who helps people to find their pigs when they lose them.

Even animals are worshipped also.

The monkey is supposed to have power over evil spirits, the tiger to preserve little children from danger, and so offerings are made to them. The viceroys and high mandarins in many parts of China worship the fox. Foxes are supposed in some peculiar way to take charge of the official seals, and so they must be worshipped by the rulers of the land ; and the Dragon King, who is believed to be able to give or withhold rain when it is needed, is worshipped not only by viceroys, but by the Emperor himself.

" If you do not believe in our other gods," the Chinese say sometimes, " surely you will not deny that there is a God of Thunder ! See how he strikes people dead who have offended him." It is the common belief in China that those who are killed by lightning (or thunder, as they say) are persons who have lived evil lives and displeased the gods.

Not long ago a man who worked in an idol-maker's shop lost his life in this way. I remember when the people were discussing the matter ; they all agreed that as they did not know of anything seriously wrong in his life, he must have been a very bad person in some previous state of existence, and was thus paying the penalty for crimes committed then.

The God of Fire is always worshipped after the frequent fires which occur in every Chinese city. He is supposed, I believe, by most people, to be rather the deliverer from fire than the cause of it.

A story is told in connection with a temple erected in his honour by a former emperor after the destruction of one of his finest palaces. In the midst of the fire the Emperor declared he saw the figure of a little old man with a long white beard. Now this was considered very extraordinary, since the images of the God of Fire are always represented with red beards, and are supposed to be connected with flames of fire. The Emperor was very anxious to erect a temple in honour of the god, whom he feared he had offended; so he ordered his attendants to go to every temple in the city and try and discover the God of Fire who had a white beard. This was a difficult matter, and all the principal temples in the city were searched without success. At last, in a dilapidated temple outside one of the city gates, it was found that there was in existence an idol which, being minus a beard, had been supplied with one made of frayed-out hemp.

The case was reported to the Emperor, who visited the ruined temple in great state, doing reverence before the image, and vowing that he would build for it a temple as fine as any in the city.

The new building was erected on the site of the neglected ruined shrine.

The God of War is worshipped by many others as well as soldiers, for they believe that he will make them strong and courageous. So lately as 1855 they say he appeared before the imperial troops and led them to victory over the rebels; and since then they have raised him to higher rank among the gods than before.

Nearly every trade in China has its special patron, but the God of Wealth is honoured by merchants of every rank. His image, set in a small niche with incense burning before it, is seen in most Chinese shops, and he is believed to help his worshippers to become speedily rich.

The Goddess of Mercy, Ma-Chu, the Goddess of Sailors, and an idol called "Mother," have a large number of worshippers, especially among women and children. When there is a storm at sea, or on one of the great lakes or rivers of China, the sailors cry piteously for mercy to the "Venerable Mother Ma-Chu," who, they believe, will come to their rescue.

The original of the goddess, if we may be allowed that term, died when a girl of twenty. During her lifetime she told a wonderful story of a remarkable dream she had. Her father and brothers were seafaring men, and, while anxiously expecting their return, she dreamed she was out at sea watching three junks in great danger. She seized two of them in either hand, and the third she held between her teeth, and swimming thus, she had almost reached a haven of safety. But, hearing her mother call to her, she felt compelled to answer, and so loosed her hold upon the third boat, and awaking found it was a dream. But some days after the brothers returned, telling of the wonderful deliverance of their two junks by an invisible power, and how their father's boat was wrecked when almost within sight of land. It was evident to all who heard the story that Ma-Chu, without knowing it, was possessed of miraculous power, and since her death the honour due to a goddess has been paid to her.

Little boys and girls are very early taught to worship the goddess called "Mother," who, with a large number of attendants, is supposed carefully to watch over children and protect them through the diseases of infancy.

I have told you much about the gods of China, in which so many millions of the Chinese place their trust; but some of the wisest men of the nation have little faith in them. Yet every one believes in the necessity for worshipping the spirits of their ancestors if they would be prosperous in life. As I said before, every man is believed to have three souls; one, at death, enters the spirit tablet— a sort of carved cabinet with tiny folding doors, containing a small wooden tablet upon which the deceased person's name is written.

People will occasionally be found who laugh at idol worship and have little faith in most superstitious observances, and yet they believe firmly in the necessity for, and possibility of, supplying the needs of departed relatives by placing constant offerings before the spirit tablet.

Sometimes a priest will inform a family that their friend in the unseen world is in great difficulties. They must send him large sums of money, and religious services must be held for several days. In their anxiety and grief they listen to all the priest tells them.

A service of this kind took place one day in the garden of a house quite near to us. The father of a little boy I knew well had died about a year before, and it was his spirit that the priests said was in trouble. The poor boy, who was his father's eldest son, was the principal actor in the ceremonies. He was a bright, intelligent little fellow, but it will be long before I forget the look of terror that was in the child's face as, dressed in his white mourning robes, he followed the directions of the priests and bowed rapidly at frequent intervals, while incense and paper money were burned, gongs beaten and crackers exploded.

Besides what may be strictly called religious observances, the Chinese have many strange and superstitious customs. It is not proper in China to have walls frequently whitewashed, for white is the colour of mourning; it is very rash to have windows in a house, lest they should afford ingress to evil spirits.

If your front door faces a street or lane, you must be sure and erect a wall or wooden screen immediately opposite to it, to prevent evil spirits from finding an entrance. Roads in China are rarely made straight, but wind and twist in a most wearying and perplexing manner, for it is believed spirits have an objection to these winding paths, while on the broad straight way they will certainly be met with.

When there is an eclipse of the sun or moon in China, it is well known that although the coming event is announced beforehand in the Chinese almanacs, it is nevertheless believed by many that the phenomenon is caused by an attempt on the part of an animal known as the Heavenly Dog, to eat up the luminary. The common people seem thoroughly convinced that it is a time of very real danger, and make a most terrible noise with gongs and cymbals till the eclipse

SERVICE FOR THE BENEFIT OF THE DEAD.

passes over and they believe their efforts have proved effectual, and the Heavenly Dog has been frightened away.

This "Dog" is the source of considerable anxiety to them in another connection. One summer evening, when I had not been long in China, my curiosity was aroused by the sudden bursting out of a perfect babel of sounds from the quiet streets which skirted the Mission compound. Gongs were beaten, crackers exploded, and most of the domestic utensils of iron or tin-ware were taken out and utilised to add to the universal din. I called our servant to inquire the cause, and was informed that the note of the nine-headed bird had been heard in our neighbourhood, and everybody was in fear lest it should rest upon their house. This bird was said to have originally possessed ten heads, but one of them had long ago been bitten off by that notorious Heavenly Dog. The wound has never healed, and as the bird flies along, if it chances to rest upon a house, the blood dripping from it dooms it to destruction by fire. No wonder, when the distant croak of what was probably some solitary owl was heard, the superstitious people, fearing for the safety of their homes, seized on every available article and spared no pains in making a din sufficient to drive any bird away from their neighbourhood.

So do the Chinese people seem to spend their lives from the cradle to the grave, in constant fear of unseen and often imaginary enemies. They spend large sums of money in purchasing charms which are sold by the Tauist priest, and are constantly seeking by numberless devices to keep at bay the spirits of evil which they believe are ever striving to do them harm.

CHAPTER X.

I HAVE told you what strange superstitions the Chinese have about the powers which they fancy are able to influence men's lives. You have heard how the children are taught to bow down and worship grim idols of wood and stone, of which terrible stories are told, and have never dreamed of a God who loves little children, watching over them with tenderest care.

We go to China to tell not only the grown-up men and women but also the boys and girls, the good news which we have known ever since we could understand anything—the news that we have a Father in heaven, who loves us so much that He gave His only begotten Son, that whosoever believeth in Him might not perish, but have everlasting life.

Perhaps you would like to know how we teach these Chinese boys and girls. First of all we have to win their confidence, and make the fathers and mothers as well as the children less afraid of us. For when we first go into a Chinese city many of the boys and girls will run away and hide themselves, afraid lest we should catch them and do some dreadful thing to them. Some of them will run after us, calling Yang-kwei-tsz, which means something like "foreign evil spirit" and other bad names, and a few will pick up stones and throw them at us, trying thus to drive us away.

"But why are they angry when they see us coming into their cities?" you will ask, "and why are they afraid of us?" Principally because we are not Chinamen, and have come from another country. The Chinese very much dislike people of other countries coming and trading, or having any other dealings with them, and most of them would be very glad if we were all driven out of China to-morrow. Englishmen and other foreigners would not have got into the country at all if it had not been for a great war which we had with them. England was victorious, and so she obliged China to open several of her ports to trade with foreigners, and to allow them to live there. And ever since, all that our nation or any other has gained from China has always been at the point of the sword, or because they were afraid of us. So it is only natural that they are not very pleased to see us walking about the streets of their cities.

There is another reason for their disliking us, and a still sadder one. There is a plant which grows over vast tracts of land in India, which you know belongs to England. It is a very innocent-looking flower, and is called the poppy. Perhaps it has done more harm than any other flower that ever grew. There is a juice that oozes from the capsules of this flower which, when dry, becomes opium, a powerful drug which millions of people in China are smoking to-day. They never sit up to smoke it, but lie down on a couch. It often gives them very strange and beautiful dreams, and so they are tempted to try it again. Before very long they find they can much more easily do without food or clothing than without their smoke of opium, and at last, when all they possess has been pawned and sold, they will even sell their wives and children to get more opium. Their faces get very haggard-looking, their eyes sunken, so that you know a confirmed opium smoker directly you meet him in the street.

It is very sad to think that this drug that does so much harm is sent to China by Englishmen, since India belongs to them. A great deal of opium is grown in China now, for the Chinese farmers find it pays so much better than their other crops. But when England stops sending the Indian opium—which we hope she soon will do—then the best men in China will do all they can to stop the growth of it in their own land, which they see is being ruined by it. "Where do you come from?" the Chinese often ask missionaries, and when they answer "From England," we see a sneer on their faces, and they say,

"England! Ah, that is the country that sends the opium to kill our people!" So you see there are several reasons why the Chinese do not give us a very warm welcome. And since they do not like us, the officials have from the first circulated some very wicked and untrue stories about us. They say we have very powerful and efficacious medicines, and large numbers who attend our Mission hospitals know this to be true, but they add that we make these medicines out of the eyes of people who become Christians, and from the bones of little Chinese babies. No wonder then that people are afraid to let their children come near us lest they should never see them again.

We try to win their friendship in many ways. Having learnt their language, we are soon able to say a few kind words to the children, and then we often give them some little English pictures, which delight them very much. After a while we are able to go and see their mothers in their own homes, and then they will come and see us, being curious to look at the strange things they find in our houses. What a number of questions they always have to ask us! "Is there a sun and a moon in your country?" they inquire. "Are there hills and trees?" "Why do you not have black eyes like ours? Have they faded out?" "Can you see with them several feet down into the earth, and know where gold and silver is lying?" "Why do Englishwomen have such large feet, just like men, instead of 'golden lilies' three inches long?" "Why do you wear your hair in such a strange fashion, instead of having it glued down on wire shapes?" "Why do foreign ladies wear coverings over their heads when they go out of doors? It is just like the men!" These and very many more questions are constantly asked and answered. Then sometimes we sing to them English hymns that have been translated into Chinese, such as "Jesus loves me," "There is a happy land," and many more. We show them pictures too of scenes in the life of Christ, and tell them a great deal about Him. After a while they begin to think perhaps the bad reports they have heard are not quite true.

"I have often thought of coming, with my daughter, to see you," said a mandarin's wife to me, "but I felt so much afraid of you that

I always put it off.   I shall have no fear in future, for I think you are, after all, not so very unlike ourselves."   This is how, step by step, we

BOATS ON THE YANG-TSE RIVER.

get the people to come around us, and at last to allow their children to attend our schools.

It is much easier to do this when we are settled in a large town ; but there are many millions of people in China who have never heard of Jesus and His salvation, and many cities which have never been visited by a missionary. So sometimes during the spring and autumn seasons we go and visit some of the towns that have no settled missionary, and try to tell the good news, and to sell Christian books to people who frequently have never before had an opportunity of hearing the Gospel preached. We usually take these trips in small native boats. The arched roof is of matting, tarred, to keep out the rain, and it is so low that we cannot stand quite upright in it. We are favoured with two small windows, but they are filled up with thin sheets of oyster-shells instead of glass. By taking away one of the movable boards, we can make an opening, through which we creep on to the little bit of deck. Sometimes, when sitting inside our boat, this opening serves as a window, through which we get pretty peeps at the beautiful river scenery, or glimpses of passing junks.

The inside of our boat is furnished with two stools, and the raised locker serves us for table by day and bedstead at night. Our bedding does not take up much room, since it consists only of *pukais*, or wadded quilts, such as the Chinese use. And a comfortable bed it makes, when one is snugly rolled up in it, in Chinese fashion.

Our Chinese servant is sitting in the boat, on guard. He cooks all our meals for us at a tiny charcoal stove on board, belonging to the boatman. When we reach a large country town, Mr. Bryson goes on shore, and preaches or sells books in the streets and market-places. Sometimes he is accompanied by a missionary friend, who travels in another small boat, and sometimes by a native Christian, who is very glad to tell his fellow-countrymen of what Jesus has done for him.

But what crowds of women and children come to the boat to see me ! The boys climb up on the side of it, and small black eyes watch me curiously through many a crack and hole, as if I were some wonderful wild animal on view for their amusement. After a while the women muster up courage, and one after another creeps into the boat, or crouches down on the tiny deck, and listens to what I have to tell them.   Then the little boys and girls come forward, and are made happy with an English picture or a text card.   At last so many come running from the city to our quiet anchorage, that the boatman gets alarmed.   He is afraid too many will crowd on to the boat, and it

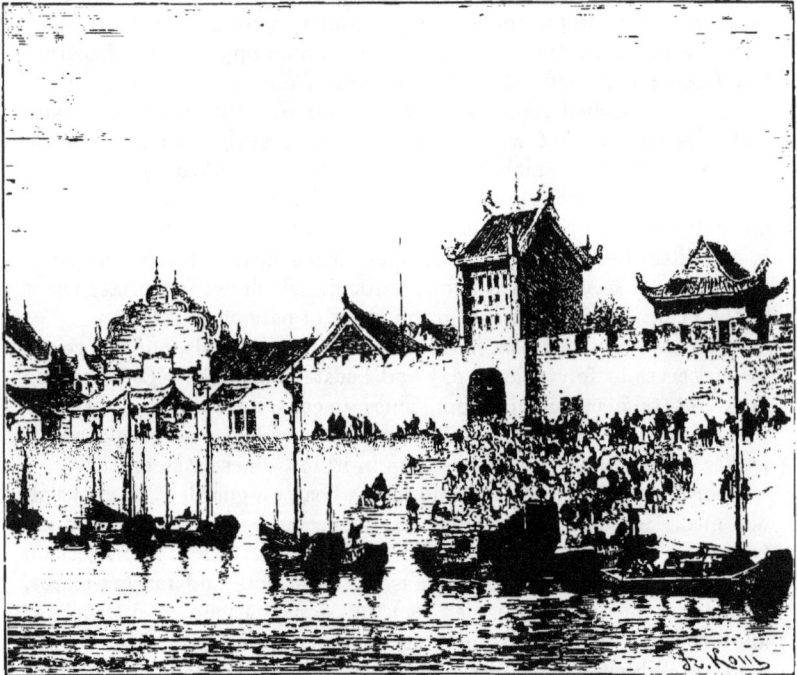

ARRIVAL OF A FOREIGNER.

will capsize. So he puts out farther from the shore. Then the people hire ferry-boats, and crowds of them come out and surround us, especially if they happen to have heard I have a little English boy on board.

They came out in this way once at a place called Pau-ngan, situated on the shores of a beautiful lake, which looked very lovely, for the trees which adorned its banks were all clothed in the brilliant tints of autumn. On the same journey we passed on to another city called Chin-nieu, where the people became very angry with us. They threw great stones on the frail mat roof of our boat, and we had entered a narrow creek, so we were quite at their mercy. After a time they became quieter, and some were willing to buy books and listen to the preaching. At other places they were so anxious to get books that they swam across the stream to obtain them. So we go on from day to day on these country journeys, sometimes being driven away from the place, and at other times meeting with people who are very glad to see and hear us. "Is Jesus living now?" "How is it He was not born in China?" "If all this happened so long ago, how is it that we in this great Middle Kingdom have been so long in hearing of it?" These and many other questions are asked of us daily. Sometimes we hear of no results from these visits; only we know no work done for God can be in vain, and we believe He will bless the seed that is sown, and make it spring up, even though it be "after many days."

Now and then, long after our visits, we hear of people who, on these occasions, for the first time heard of Jesus. They have studied the books they have bought, and then come up to the city determined to hear more of so good a religion. One earnest Christian boy heard of the Gospel first in his native town, from which the missionaries had been driven with violence. When he grew older and came to Wuchang, he found out the chapel, and before long became a true believer in Jesus, and had to endure much persecution and suffering on account of his faith.

But to go back to the city. There we have a Chinese Mission hospital, which relieves the sufferings of many thousands of people every year. One day two little girls were brought there who were believed to be quite blind. Doctor Mackenzie, who was then in charge of it, was able to perform an operation, after which they were able to see. How glad they and their parents were you can imagine!

These two girls heard about Jesus in the hospital, they learned to believe in Him, and are now living happy Christian lives in their village homes.

A boy was brought to the hospital who was suffering very great pain because he had performed what in China is considered a meritorious action. His father was ill, and, hoping to cure him, he had actually cut a piece of flesh out of his own leg, and given it to his father among his other food, hoping that he would recover from his sickness. Very many filial sons do this in China : they are told if they do it, " with a pure heart," their parents will certainly recover. This poor boy was very ill indeed for a long time. Another boy, who was the son of a mandarin living in a city farther down the river, was brought to the hospital by his mother, who was on a visit to the town. He recovered from his illness, and having heard much about Jesus in the hospital, and from Mr. Owen, who used to teach him every night, he determined to become a Christian. I remember him well on the last Sunday before he left to return to his heathen home. How happy he looked, singing the glad Christian hymns in the chapel ! He was going, like Joseph, far away from all who loved and worshipped the God he had chosen. But He who kept Joseph faithful in the dark land of Egypt could keep this Chinese boy through the trials he would certainly have to endure.

I told you how, by degrees, we were able to get people to allow their children to come to our schools. Let me tell you a little about them, and the lessons they learn. We always try to obtain a Christian master, who is also a good scholar. The children get a very good Chinese education, and, in addition, they study the Bible and Catechism. They have wonderfully good memories, and I think you would find they could surpass most English children, if they were set to learn the same lesson by heart. Many of them think nothing of repeating several chapters, or even a whole Gospel from memory ; and not long ago, in a Mission school in North China, they had a boy who could repeat the whole of the New Testament through without mistake.

I should like you to hear some of our Chinese children singing. They have not very musical voices in Central China, neither had they for a long time the least idea of time. But they do thoroughly enjoy singing their hymns, many of which are translations of those you sing here in England.

During the great examination season, when some ten thousand students come up from all parts of the province to compete for their degree, it is a very busy time in the city of Wuchang.

The parents of some of our boys are very poor, and they are obliged to keep them away from school for half the day, so that they may earn a little money by carrying about baskets of nuts and cakes, and selling them to the students. On one of these occasions, I was told, by some one who heard them, that while our little scholars were trying to sell their wares they took the opportunity, every now and then, to join in singing one of their school hymns. It was a new one they had just been learning—

> "In heaven there is no more sorrow;
> There is no more death and pain."

The strange sounds gathered a little crowd around the boys. "Where did you learn that song?" asked a grave elderly man, wearing large spectacles in heavy tortoise-shell frames, giving him, in Chinese eyes, a most learned appearance. "We were taught it at the Glad Tidings Hall," replied the children. "It sounds very strange, and yet there is something attractive in it," said another student. "It is extraordinary that the foreigners should teach children anything like that."

We were pleased to hear that our boys had been trying to sing for Jesus, for we know how glad He is to receive the services of children, even in their earliest days.

Others, we know, repeat the lessons they have learned at school in their own homes; and some are teaching their little friends much of what they learn. One of our boys, named Tsz-Sz-Heu, had a number of little friends who were not allowed by their parents to come to the Christian school. He used, after leaving school, to tell the

other boys the Bible stories he had heard there.   One day, Mr.
Bryson was surprised to see a number of strange boys' faces peeping
into the chapel adjoining the school-room, where he had been
preaching. The remarkable thing about them was, that these boys
did not seem at all afraid of him, as most heathen boys would have
been. He began talking to the children, and was much surprised
when one little boy said, " We know it is wrong to worship idols. The
God we must serve is our Father in heaven, who sent His Son to die
for us." They went on to say, that since every one had done wrong,
and all have sinned, and must be punished, Jesus died, and those who
believe in Him are saved, and live for ever in heaven. " And who
taught you all this ? " the children were asked. They replied that it
was their little friend, our scholar. Tsz-Sz-Heu was by no means one
of our brightest boys, and we were much encouraged to find that he
had himself become a little missionary, and was teaching his young
companions the truths he had learned in the school.

Christmas Day is always a holiday long looked forward to by our
school children, for then we have a grand feast, and prizes are distributed.   How busy they are all the day before, gathering and
collecting evergreens to adorn the school-room. Then a large number
of coloured Scripture pictures are arranged round the walls, and here
and there pairs of scarlet Chinese scrolls are hung up, bearing a text,
or having some suitable motto written upon them.

Among the native Christians there was one man who had once
belonged to a wealthy family, in a far distant province.   He had
wasted all his money, and was in very poor circumstances, when he
came to our city and heard the Gospel first. He could write or paint
the strange Chinese characters most beautifully, and had been
accustomed at the New Year's season to earn a great deal of money
by writing scrolls intended to serve idolatrous or superstitious
purposes. He was requested to write many such after he heard the
Gospel. He had not become a member of the Church, but his reply
was, " No ; I have decided to join the Christians. I can have nothing
to do with anything connected with idolatry."   Here is one of the

mottoes he wrote for the school treat. "The birthday of Him who brought joy to men of every land."

Our reading desk was adorned with fragrant lemons peeping out among their glossy leaves; then there were "heavenly bamboos," with their brilliant berries and many other plants.

When Christmas morning came, you may be sure the children and their parents were all there in very good time, attired in their best clothing, in honour of the day. First we sang a hymn. It was " Hark the herald angels sing," in Chinese, of course; then, after-prayer, the beautiful story of the Babe of Bethlehem was read, followed by a Christmas address from the pastor, which seemed to be full of interest to the smallest children. After the conclusion of the service the prizes were given out. What an exciting moment it was, for parents as well as children, when one child after another came up to receive the prize allotted to him!

Everyone was made happy with something, though all the gifts were not of equal value. Here were some gay little Chinese caps, —just the thing for the New Year's season, which was so soon coming on. Here were some lead pencils and pocket-knives, which had been sent out from England by some kind friends of Chinese children. Here were books filled with pictures, which would give the children and their friends pleasure for many a long day to come.

When every child had received a present, it was about time for the feast to commence. You would have been surprised to see how fast the chopsticks go to work, and how quickly the rice basins need refilling. Eight children sit at each table. In the centre of every table stands a basin of stewed fish or meat, as the case may be. Every boy helps himself as he feels inclined, according to Chinese custom, out of this centre dish, but each child has a rice basin to him or herself. Beside the day school, we have a Sunday school, which is attended by all the week-day scholars and as many others as they can persuade to come with them by holding out the promise of a little English picture to be given by the teacher.

Some of the older lads have left school and are now in situations.

They have received permission from their masters to attend the school, but unfortunately the number who are thus allowed to come is very small.

The school is opened just like Sunday schools at home with singing and prayer, and then the teachers, who are all members of the Church, take their separate classes and go over the same lesson, which most of them have prepared with the pastor in the early morning of the previous day. When teaching-time is over, a coloured illustration of the lesson for the day is hung upon the blackboard, and the children are questioned upon what they have been taught.

Quite a forest of hands goes up as a proof that they can answer nearly every question; and I think that English children who were studying the same lesson would have to be very attentive, or they would find the Chinese boys and girls could pass the examination more successfully than they.

It is more difficult to get girls to our school than boys, but those who come, if only allowed to attend regularly, we find quite as bright and intelligent as their brothers. Before the principal festivals of the year, we always speak very earnestly to the children about the sin of idolatry, for we know they will see so much of it around them on every hand.

After one New Year's holiday we found that some of our boys had been to several of the idol shrines, and pulling out the sticks of incense burning before them, had thrown them away. In one small temple they had knocked down one or two small figures of the attendants of the idol, to show the people they were of no use, and no one need be afraid of them. But of course we had to condemn such lawless proceedings.

Some who were scholars when we first commenced the school are now almost young men.

One of them is hoping to become a preacher of the Gospel; some are in situations in places of business, or in service, and are trying to live as Christians.

PART II.

CHAPTER I.

YAU-TING; OR, FIRST-FRUITS GATHERED.

ONE day in mid-autumn, some twenty years ago, the streets of a grand old city in Central China were all astir with busy life. Some of the bright-coloured sign-boards had been adorned with a new coat of paint, and most of the tradesmen had a brisk business-like air about them, as if times were good and trade flourishing. If you had gone out of the main thoroughfares into the more retired streets you would have seen large red bills pasted above the doorways, intimating that within there were apartments to let for the "Senior Wrangler." For what young student in need of apartments could resist the attraction of such an advertisement? All these were signs that the great Triennial Examinations were in progress, and the city had been making preparations to receive her ten thousand guests. These scholars had come up from all parts of the province, with the hope of obtaining in the competitive examinations the degree which is the passport in China to official rank and honour.

Not only was young China represented there, gay in robes of delicate-coloured silks and *crêpes*, but there were venerable men also, with snowy locks and forms bent with age. They had entered in many a contest, and failed to receive the prize which only sixty-one in ten thousand can obtain, but they were determined to try again,

K

since they considered the honour more than sufficient reward for all the toil and pains spent in striving after it.

It was at this time that a respectable middle-aged man might have been seen passing along one of these crowded streets. At last he stopped before the shop of a dealer in fancy wares and needlework, and might have been seen gazing through the open shop-front at some of the beautiful handiwork exhibited there. Here were squares of gorgeous scarlet, embroidered with beautiful sprays of flowers, which are in great request as marriage presents. Ladies' head-dresses were there also in great variety. A sort of band or coronet to encircle the head was the foundation in all cases; but while some were elaborately embroidered, others were studded with little ornaments not unlike tiny brooches. Beside them were caps for boys, of various bright colours, adorned with gay silk tassels; daintily embroidered purses, and a variety of other small articles.

The master of the establishment had a large number of *employées* among the poor women of the neighbourhood, who helped to keep their households beyond the reach of want by their skilful and beautiful handiwork.

The man who had been looking at all the varied show of ornamental needlework soon entered the shop. He wished to purchase a spectacle case, and after much talking and bargaining the business was concluded. Then, to his dismay, the customer discovered that he had not with him sufficient money to pay for his purchase. Looking round, he saw, playing near to him, a little dark-eyed boy about seven years of age. Yau-ting was the little fellow's name; he was a bright lively child, and the pet of the household. The purchaser turned to the assistant who had served him, and apologising for the dilemma in which he found himself, suggested that the boy should accompany him to his home, which was not very far off, and receive payment for the spectacle case. With the ready politeness which is so characteristic of the Chinese, the offer was accepted, and the middle-aged man and the little boy might soon have been seen walking side by side through the busy streets.

In the meantime, the father of the child had returned home, and being busily engaged in attending to customers, failed to notice the absence of his little son. "Where is Yau-ting?" he inquired after a while, expecting to hear that the little fellow was playing with some of his childish companions.

"Yau-ting," repeated the assistant, and there was a look of dismay upon his face, "why, I thought he had returned long ago."

"Where did you think he would return from?" asked the unsuspecting father.

"Why, he went away almost an hour ago with a customer who came from the Glad Tidings Hall, which has been lately opened in the city."

The father's face grew pale with fear, and he turned sharply upon the young man. "You dared to send my son into that infamous place! You, who have heard how the outer barbarians murder and extract the eyes of innocent children, to obtain the means for making their strangely efficacious medicines! Why, the child may be in terrible danger at this moment!" and unable to endure the thought of the tragedy which his fancy pictured, the father rushed from the house, determined to do everything in his power to rescue his child from the hands of those who were connected with the terrible barbarians!

Meanwhile, the mother and the other members of the family having heard that the hope of the house had been spirited away by a member of the hated "Jesus religion," wept and bewailed as if the news of the little one's death had already reached them. And the father, heedless of the busy life of the crowded thoroughfares, careless of the coolies hastening on with their heavy loads, unconscious of everything but his child's danger, saw and heard nothing till he reached the "Glad Tidings Hall of the Jesus religion." It was an ordinary Chinese building, merely a shop turned into a preaching hall. He would never have dreamed of entering the place at any other time; but now his child was there, and, father-like, his only thought was how he might rescue him. He entered, and the first sight he saw was the small Yau-ting happily playing with another Chinese boy of about the same age.

The teacher who was in charge of the hall, and in whose company the child had left his home, advanced towards him. He politely invited him to enter the guest room and drink tea there, apologising at the same time for detaining the little lad so long, because he was anxious to remain with his new-found playfellow. At any other time I have no doubt Mr. Fan would have most certainly declined the invitation. He would have feared that any beverage offered to him in such a place might not be tea at all, but the "medicine of bewilderment," which it was said changed men's thoughts and lives, and made them "willing to do anything the Jesus people said was right."

But, with his heart filled with the sense of relief that the sight of his precious little son had given him, he was for the moment oblivious of all evil reports. He sat down with the teacher Pau, and drank of the tea he offered, while they smoked together the pipe of friendship. Although he did not remain long, before leaving Mr. Fan had promised to call again, and had invited the teacher to his own home. Mr. Pau politely accompanied his visitor to the door, begging him to "walk slowly," apologising meanwhile, in Chinese fashion for scant hospitality. Mr. Fan replied with the usual polite expressions, and holding the hand of his little son, made his way home with a grateful heart.

The whole family welcomed the little wanderer, and rejoiced together as they laughed at their previous fears. And in the teacher's home there was gladness too that night. The poor teacher, whose life was by no means an easy one, since he was the sole witness for Jesus in all that great city. He might have become used to the jeers of common people, and the sneers of the haughty *literati*, but constant repetition did not make him feel their scornful words any the less. The proud disciples of Confucius were constantly inquiring what he meant by his presumptuous attempt to aid "the barbarians," by helping them in spreading the doctrines of the "unknown Western teacher, called Jesus," among those who were followers of China's revered sage.

Human nature finds it hard to grow accustomed to these things, and day after day, as this lonely servant of Christ closed the doors of the preaching hall, while the evening shadows were darkening in the narrow streets, his heart sunk within him. Despised and rejected, hated by all, truly like many another Christian in China to-day, he had to take up his cross and follow his Divine Master very closely along the path of trial and suffering. One, who was in all points tempted even as His servants are, pitied the weary heart of His faithful follower, and sent this ray of sunshine to brighten his lonely way.

The adventures of small Yau-ting served as a link to bind together his own and the teacher's family. They exchanged frequent visits, and the Christian teacher had many opportunities of commending the truths he believed to the notice of his new friends. The women of the families became acquainted also, and the teacher's wife was indeed glad as she told her heathen sister of One who is the Friend of women in every land.

Time passed on, and Yau-ting's father became a believer in Jesus, and decided to cast in his lot with the despised Christians, and his wife also gave her heart to Christ. They were received into the Church, and Yau-ting, with his parents, were rarely absent from their places in the chapel when the Lord's Day came round. One of my bright memories of early days in China is the recollection of Yau-ting's happy face, as he sang with all his heart some of those well-known hymns the translations of which are as dear to Chinese as to English Christians.

The boy's seat in chapel used to be between his young friend, the teacher's son, and our senior deacon, Hu. An earnest and devoted servant of the Lord was Hu, one whose constant desire it was to tell those who had never heard it the glad tidings which had filled his own life with joy. Two of that little trio are no longer members of the Church militant. They stand before the throne, a part of that great multitude which no man can number, who shall come out of every kingdom, and people, and tongue, who are coming now from the "Land of Sinim."

The next great event which I remember in the life of young Yau-ting was his marriage. He was only a lad of sixteen or so, but Chinese custom betroths babies, and marries girls and boys. I saw the boy-bridegroom on his wedding day, at the marriage feast, to which we were invited. Very bright and handsome he looked, attired in the grand robes of a high official, which may be worn on his marriage day by every Chinese bridegroom. In accordance with the usual custom, he handed round several dishes to the guests invited to the feast, and then retired. The little bride was not so pleasant-looking as her boy-husband. Her face was sadly scarred with small-pox, but she had a gentle and grave expression of countenance. She used to come with her mother-in-law and little sister to my weekly Bible class, and would watch, my every movement with frightened questioning eyes. No wonder, poor child; for she had doubtless heard many terrible stories in her country home of the hated foreigners, and could not at once place in us so much confidence as she saw the rest of the family did. Gradually, and by slow degrees, the trembling, girlish heart was won, not only to regard the foreign teachers with friendliness, but, best of all, to love and reverence the Lord Jesus as her Saviour; and after a time of probation she was received into the fellowship of the little band of Christians. Her husband had professed his faith in Christ some months before.

I always remember the happy day when Yau-ting with his young friend, the teacher's son, made a profession of their faith. Two lads they were, with the brightness of youth upon their faces, both were the sons of Christians, and it was a glad sight to see them putting on the armour. With full hearts we united with the little band of Chinese converts in praying that they might be kept faithful, through life, even unto death.

A year or so after, a little grandchild was born into the family.

Christianity does not immediately change and obliterate the habits and thoughts derived from generations of heathen ancestors, and it was a great disappointment to the family to receive into their midst a granddaughter instead of the longed-for grandson. But the little girl was tenderly loved and cared for. The day on which she was baptised, being held in the arms of her delighted grandmother, seems to me, when I look back, almost the last season of great gladness which fell to the lot of the Fan family. Not that their daily life previously had been free from trials and persecutions. It is impossible, at present, for Christians to live in China unmolested by their neighbours, who look upon them, if not with hatred, with suspicious fear. Taxes in aid of idolatrous ceremonies are constantly levied; and when the Christians refuse to contribute to such objects, they have to endure many insults, if not attacks which endanger life and limb.

At the grand idol festivals, which are held on frequent occasions throughout the year, the Christians are marked men. Their attendance upon the Sabbath services makes them the butt not only of the laughter and ridicule, but for the scandals and evil-speaking of the neighbourhood in which they live. But these are only the common trials of all Chinese converts.

How different in the foundation of its teaching is the religion of Jesus when compared with all heathen faiths! If you worship the gods, riches and honour, and long life and prosperity shall attend you, is the teaching of most false religions. "Whom the Lord loveth He chasteneth, and scourgeth every son whom He receiveth," is the testimony of the Word of God.

And for the Fan family a time of trial, which was to test their faith to the utmost, was indeed at hand. The father became seriously ill, and day by day he grew weaker. The best native medical advice was procured, and many remedies tried, but without success. He was unwilling to leave his home and enter the English hospital which was on the other side of the Yang-tse river, but he thankfully received the foreign medicines provided for him; and his family nursed him tenderly, more in accordance with Western ideas than with Chinese plans for sick nursing. But the disease had taken too strong a hold upon him to be checked, and through the hot days of midsummer he grew weaker and weaker, and at last passed quietly away to his rest. There was a look of such perfect peace upon the still face as it lay in the coffin, that it was remarked with wondering surprise by all the heathen neighbours who had been invited in to take a last look, and to assure themselves that the reports about taking out the eyes of dead Christians were quite unfounded. How strange it all seemed to them ! There was no wild tumult of weeping in the death-chamber, but amid the natural grief of widow and orphan was the hopeful looking forward to a glad meeting in a land beyond the grave.

There was no burning of incense or paper money, no worship before the spirit tablet, no calling in of priests to rid the house of evil spirits. It was all perplexing beyond measure.

The young Yau-ting had at once to take up his position as head of the Christian family, with all the trials and difficulties inseparably connected with it. He was a lad of bright promise, with all his father's charm of amiability and kindliness, and also a decision and strength of character which his father had never possessed. Was it wonderful that we expected great things of him ? Is it strange that we believe he is now engaged in a nobler service yonder ?

For in the bright morning of his days the disease which h as called so many away from the dear shores of England, was sent as the messenger to call him home from the crowded Eastern city. He was attacked by consumption, and although every care was lavished upon him, and earnest prayers rose constantly on his behalf, it was not the will of the Father to spare him longer. We could see that he was slowly but surely failing. How happy he used to look at the services in the little Chinese chapel—for he attended them to the very last ! It was a touching group indeed : the widowed mother, the young wife, and the little daughter, and the hope of the family passing away from them for ever.

It was on the 9th of February, 1882, that the summons came. He received it surrounded by a little band of Christian friends, who commended him into the hands of the Saviour he loved. " I know that Jesus is with me," were some of his last words. Then calling to his side his widowed mother, soon to be bereaved of her only son, he begged her not to grieve for him, but whatever trials she might have to endure—and his loving heart told him they would not be light or few—never, under any circumstances, to forsake Christ, or give up her confidence in Him. Soon after, his spirit passed away to the Saviour in whom he trusted. He was laid to rest in the burying-ground of our infant Church. Just outside the eastern gate of the city, almost overshadowed by the grim walls of an ancient heathen temple, all that was mortal of Yau-ting lies sleeping till the Resurrection morning.

Prosperity and long life, say the heathen, is the lot of those who worship at the idol shrines ; and even to our dim, earthly eyes it seems at times as if it would surely have been well that the young Christian should have been left to fight his Lord's battles in the land where the soldiers of Christ are so few. But God's ways are not as our ways. He has called Yau-ting to the higher service above ; his short, bright life is over, but the memory of it lives in many a heart that loved him.

CHAPTER II.

In a village in the Han-chwan district, about one hundred miles from the mart of Hankow, there lived some years ago a family of the name of Hu.

The father was the possessor of a small piece of land, which he cultivated himself, and he also followed the trade of a barber. This business is one which is held in no very high repute in China, although the people are more dependent than the men of other nations upon the services of that fraternity. Indeed, the followers of this calling, together with actors and mandarins' attendants, are prohibited from competing in the great literary examinations, by means of which the son of the poorest peasant, if successful, may attain to the highest offices of state.

Hu was a man of high rank, however, from a religious point of view, for he bore upon his head the marks of the ordination ceremony, which is performed upon lay brethren as well as those who have separated themselves from all secular affairs. And yet—strange paradox as it sounds to Christian ears—although his position as a follower of Buddha was so high, he was one of the worst characters in the village. He was a man of whom his neighbours stood in fear, and he was the leader in much that was evil.

At last, a preacher of the strange new faith of the foreigners, called the "Jesus religion," came to this Hupeh village, and Hu, the reprobate, heard the glad tidings of One who died that sinners might have life. His heart was touched, and he sought and found forgiveness for his sin-stained past at the feet of Him who, in far-off

Galilee, was known as "the Friend of publicans and sinners." His whole life was altered; he forsook his old evil habits, and his changed behaviour was the talk of the country-side. He became anxious to unite himself publicly with the followers of Jesus; and in June, 1874, he was received into the Church by baptism.

Before this he had decided, to the great dismay of all his heathen friends, to destroy by burning what, in their eyes, was a most precious and sacred document. It was the certificate of his ordination, and was thought to represent so high a degree of merit, that large sums of money could have been readily obtained for it. That their neighbour Hu should so recklessly forfeit all claim to this vast amount of accumulated merit seemed to these villagers not only an act of desecration but of foolish wastefulness. Yet it made them speculate curiously as to wherein lay the attraction and power of this new religion, which changed men's lives and made them willing to endure persecution and loss rather than give up their faith. A faith, too, whose object seemed to be that unknown Western Sage, who, because He came from the West, must necessarily be inferior to any holy man who had been born within the boundaries of the great Celestial Empire.

There was such a change in Hu's household after he became a Christian, that it was not wonderful to find his wife was attracted by it. She willingly listened while he told her of that Saviour who, strange as it sounds to Chinese ears, died for women as well as their husbands, and offers His salvation as freely to the daughters as the sons of men. As she heard, her heart was opened, like Lydia's, and she became a follower of Jesus also; and the little daughter of the household found there was a message for her as well.

Shin-Ku, or the "New Daughter," was the name she bore. I wish I could show you her portrait, but that has never yet been taken. Picture, then, a bright-faced Chinese lassie, with raven hair, that used to be gathered up into a long thick plait, which hung down her back, and was tied at the end with a bright scarlet cord. She wore a dress that never varied much, either in shape or colour. It consisted of a little tunic of blue cotton, occasionally trimmed with pretty bands of silk ribbon, and pantalettes of the same material, ornamented in a similar way. Her dark eyes grew bright with interest, as she listened to the sweet story of the Saviour who placed His hands on little children's heads and claimed them for His own. How different it was from the tales of the idols, worshipped in Chinese temples, which always filled her heart with fear and dread!

Shin-Ku always remembers that day in autumn when she left her quiet village home in company with her mother and aunt and some other friends, sailing down the swift waters of the Han till they reached the great city where some of their relatives resided. On they went for many a mile down the fine stream which comes from a distance of more than a thousand miles, flowing from the far north-west of the empire. For many a mile it twisted and wound its way through the great plain, which is only occasionally diversified by a low green hill or slope of rising ground. At last they reached the place where the swift Han discharges its waters into the grand Yang-tse-kiang, giving its name to the great commercial town of Han-kow or Han's mouth. What a forest of masts there was at this junction of the two streams! There were craft of all kinds. Fine junks with ornamental sterns, laden with the productions of far Sz-chwen, and others, even more imposing, from the province of Kiang-si. Coal barges of rough build, intended to be broken up when their voyage was over, filled with coal from the mines of Hunan. All these and many more were there. Then what strange-looking houses lined the river-bank! they seemed to be standing on stilts. They were built on long piles driven into the bank, and when the Yang-tse rose and overflowed its banks, in the summer season, it seemed as if the city was running over into the river. But at the end of autumn when the waters sunk some forty feet or more, the appearance presented was odd in the extreme.

How busy were the streets of the city! They were crowded from day to day with a busy throng, and among them were strangers from almost every one of the eighteen provinces. The shops were wonderful sights indeed, with all their grand display of outfitters' stores and jewellery. The ladies' tunics were lined with the costliest furs, and ornamented with braid of cloth of gold, and the sleeves were trimmed with strips of embroidery representing fairy landscapes, and birds and insects of gorgeous tints. Then there were the shoe shops. Was it possible that there were men who wore those slippers made of delicate silks and satins? Workers in gold and silver exhibited hair ornaments, earrings, and rings of strange magnificence. And the restaurants and cook-shops, did anyone ever dream before of the wonderful delicacies there on sale? The village child was in a state of delighted bewilderment as she walked through the streets that seemed to her so strangely grand. But there was something else which interested her more than all beside, and that was the Christian services which were held in the small Chinese chapel. It made her glad to be assured there were so many more of her people who were the servants of Jesus too. When the day of rest came round, the little girl, with her relatives, joined the other Christians in their worship of the one living and true God.

It was always a glad day in the country village when one or two Christian families met together, and strove, by study of the Word of God and communion, to help each other on in the way of life. But when Shin-Ku was taken to the Hankow Chapel and saw the place crowded on the Sabbath morning with men and women who had professed their faith in Christ,—when she heard them singing with heart and soul the praises of that Heavenly Father who gave His Son to save them, her heart overflowed with joy. Some people might have thought how small was the number of worshippers compared with the multitude of idolaters in that great city; some might have thought the sound of many untrained voices harsh and unmusical; but to Shin-Ku's childish heart it was the House of God and the very Gate of Heaven.

In December, 1876, she, with her mother and aunt, was received into the Church by baptism; not in the central chapel of the great city, but in the smaller meeting-place of Hanyang, where her relatives then

resided. Soon after, the little party returned to the quiet village by
the Han river, and the days in the busy town were remembered as a
pleasant dream. Not as a dream only; for the good seed which had
been sown in her country home had been watered and quickened into
vigorous life during that visit, and was now bearing fruit.

What a happy life she led, although quite uneventful! In the
bright summer days came the time of the cotton harvest, when most
of the women and children of the village went out into the fields to
pick the snow-white balls of down just peeping from the pods. Everybody enjoyed that time, from the small maiden of two or three
summers, who liked to imitate her elders and fill her tiny tunic with
the downy treasures, to the aged grand-dame bent with the weight
of years, who was almost too old for work, but loved to sit in the
pleasant sunshine and listen to the cheery gossip of the cotton-pickers.
Shin-Ku enjoyed it too, although she had frequently to bear many
unkind slights from her neighbours. They often called her and her
friends by unkind names, for they were angry, because instead of
worshipping at the idol shrines, they loved and reverenced One whose
very name they hated. For those who love darkness rather than light
have associated the name of Jesus in China with fearful stories of
deeds of violence, and terrible atrocities which exist only in their
imagination. No wonder the unlearned country people are terrified at
the thought of anyone connected with them embracing this mysterious
faith. " They know not what they do," was our Lord's compassionate
verdict upon the maddened crowd which called out " Crucify Him ! " in
the streets of Jerusalem. Are not the same pitiful words repeated
even now when He sees the great multitude of the inhabitants of the
world He died for wandering in darkness, and oftentimes when they
catch the first glimmer of the glorious Light, rejecting and turning
away from it?

Besides the cotton-picking, there were many other little duties
which kept Shin-Ku's small hands busily employed. Many silkworms were reared in the village, and the little girl had charge of
the busy workers which belonged to her father and mother. She

used to feed them with the fresh-plucked mulberry leaves, and tend them with unwearying care till the time came when they required food no longer. What a pretty sight it was, then, to see the large trays gradually filled with the soft glossy balls of a light golden colour, which seemed to take the place of her small charges!

Shin-Ku's life had been on the whole a very bright one, but a great sorrow was now threatening to overshadow it. Her loving mother, who had trained her with tender care, and made the religion she loved attractive to those who came in contact with her, began to fail in health, and before long became seriously ill. Very soon she was called away from this world.

She left her lowly peasant home without fear, for she knew that she was going to a land far brighter, and to a Friend far dearer than even those she left behind. Only one thought disturbed her, and that was the uncertainty of her little daughter's future. For in the days that were gone by, before they had heard of the religion of Jesus, they had betrothed Shin-Ku to the son of a heathen neighbour. These Chinese betrothals are as binding as a marriage, and the parents' hearts failed them as they thought of their little daughter at some future day becoming a member of a heathen family, being forced to bow down before the family shrines, and worship in the temples. This had hitherto appeared as a distant fear,—coming nearer, it was true, but still far off. But now that her mother was dead, nothing was more likely than a request from the family to which she was promised that she should at once be given up to their protection.

The father, in dismay, sent up to the provincial city of Wuchang where his brother was then living, and entreated him to try and see if some arrangement could not be made to keep Shin-Ku in a Christian home till she was some years older, and stronger to face the opposition and persecution she would certainly have to encounter in her new home. This brother was a most earnest Christian man, but poor in this world's goods. He might have been in easy circumstances had conscience allowed him to continue the old practices of his heathen life. He came to the Mission House at this time to

A VILLAGE AUDIENCE.

consult us about the matter. Very gladly I consented to take charge
of the little motherless girl, and allow her to attend our day school
in the city. But before this arrangement could be ratified by her
father, a kindly aunt who lived in the same village had offered to
undertake the care of her young niece. It was the same aunt who
on that long-to-be-remembered Sabbath-day had received baptism
together with Shin-Ku and her dear dead mother. No wonder that
the child's heart clung to her, and that she was happy in her home.

There were few exciting incidents in the life of the country village,
so it was not strange that the visits of the foreign missionary were
great events in the life of the Hu family. The father used to set
aside all business matters and give up his whole time to accompanying
the pastor, and assisting him in preaching the glad news, not only
in his own, but in many neighbouring villages. As a rule, a kindly
reception was given to them in every place, stools were brought out
of the cottages for their use, and tea was offered, as they talked
to the curious crowds, which followed wherever they went, of Jesus
and His dying love for men. As evening came on, the little band of
Christians, which was gradually increasing in the village, gathered in
the house of Shin-Ku's father. As one and another told of how,
though persecuted and despised for the dear Lord's sake, they had
been blessed and strengthened in the Christian life, it made the heart
of the pastor glad, and he thanked God and took courage. On one
occasion, while the Christians held communion together, a crowd had
gathered outside the house; some of them were noisy, and bent
upon making a disturbance, but others were anxious to learn something of the new doctrine. From dark till nearly midnight the
Christians and the pastor answered questions and explained difficulties,
till at last only a few inquirers remained.

The visitors had to be on board their boat that night, and so must
say farewell to these few sheep in the wilderness. Shin-Ku's aunt
had pressed upon the teachers a basket of her finest country eggs,
and the little girl begged with tears to be allowed to accompany them
to the river-side. But it was very late, and the boat more than a

mile distant, so the good-byes had to be said in her father's house, notwithstanding the little girl's tears and entreaties.

Though still young, Shin-Ku was felt by each member of that little company of believers to be a true Christian, with the "warm heart," by which they expressively describe those who are earnest in their faith. It filled the father's heart with joy to see his little daughter following so closely in the footsteps of her dead mother ; but whenever a thought of her betrothal came into his mind he was filled with anxious care and perplexity. After careful investigation it was found that some trivial formality had been omitted in drawing out the deeds of betrothal, and he thought that it was possible the family to which she was promised might be persuaded to give up a daughter-in-law who belonged to the despised sect of the Christians. He decided at any rate to make the proposal, and try to get the matter arranged by mutual consent. But his hopes were not to be realized. He found the lad's family determined that the betrothal should be considered binding. His heart failed him, but he told them he must insist upon the insertion of an additional clause in the marriage contract. His daughter was a Christian, and she must be all owed freedom to worship in peace the God she served. They knew she belonged to the "Jesus sect," and yet they were determined she should become a member of their family. Therefore if they failed to keep their part of the contract, and persecuted and ill-treated the child after her marriage, he should consider he was at liberty to reclaim her. The heart of the father was only partially relieved by the protestations and promises of the family, but he could do no more, and could only leave the future in God's hands. He felt at best his little daughter would have a thorny path to tread, and could only pray that she might receive strength to continue faithful, and win, by her gentleness and love, those around her to Christ.

Not long after this, the Christians of the village in which Shin-Ku lived determined to try and do what they could to help their friends in the city, who were under the necessity of rebuilding their chapel, which had been blown down by a violent storm. The girl heard their conversation, and saw the strings of cash, or the few copper coins, being brought out as offerings. "Cannot I do something?" she asked herself. " I who have received so much, cannot I do a little to help to build the house of God?" Quietly she withdrew to her own little room, and there, bending over the box which contained all her girlish treasures, she drew from the very bottom a small string of cash. Only a hundred or so in all, and amounting to not much more than sixpence in English money, but all that Shin-Ku possessed. Nearly every coin had a history. Here was one of a special reign, which had been given to her as a keepsake when cash was being counted and strung; here another she had received from a neighbour for some piece of work she had done. She carried the little string of coins into the next room with such a happy look upon her face! When she put her little offering upon the table with the other subscriptions every heart was touched.

" No; we will not take your money, child. It is all you have ; we cannot take that."

Shin-Ku's face clouded with sorrow and dismay. Would her Lord then reject the gift offered with her heart full of gratitude and love? No, He would not refuse it; and seeing how her heart was set upon making this offering, the Christians consented to take it. And of all the gifts, the fruit of much self-denial which were contributed by the little band of believers, none, I think, would win a warmer commendation from Him who said of old, of a similar offering, " She hath done what she could," than Shin-Ku's gift of love.

I cannot finish this story for you, because Shin-Ku's life is not finished yet. She lives still in the quiet Chinese village, striving in her humble way to live the Christian life amid many difficulties and trials we never dream of in England.

Do you wish to show your sympathy with her and to help her ? Then you can pray for her, and the prayers that English girls in happy Christian homes send up on her behalf will be to her, although she may never know it, a power to make her stronger to live the life of Christ, and let her light shine amid the darkness of the land that gave her birth.

CHAPTER III.

I HAD often noticed Chih Shwin's bright black eyes and intelligent face as he sat on a bench quite near to me during the Sabbath services. I had not been very long in China then; but the Chinese faces, which to any one fresh from home seem to look so very much alike, were beginning to appear as distinct and different to me as the faces of friends in dear old England; and, as I said before, Chih Shwin's was a pleasant face, and I was attracted to it from the first. I felt a great interest in him too for his father's sake—his good father, who was one of the most self-sacrificing Christians I ever knew, either in China or in any other land. He was a man who had been very clever at the numerous games of chance which are so common in China, and because he was an adept at card-playing, could often earn large sums of money by giving his advice to players. Wandering along the streets one day, with his basket filled with cases containing tapes, silks, and other small wares, he strolled out of curiosity into the preaching hall situated upon one of the busiest streets. There he heard the wonderful story of a Saviour who came "not to call the righteous, but sinners to repentance." The message which came to him that afternoon filled his thoughts and gave him no rest till he had heard more of so strange a faith. In the end he gave his heart to Christ, and every one who knew him wondered to see how the new faith could so entirely alter a man's life and habits.

After this he seemed to live only to tell others the good news that had made him glad. He was in poor circumstances, but was never tempted to use the Day of Rest for his business. When the missionary was going on a preaching trip into the country districts, Chih Shwin's father would often ask to be allowed to accompany him, that he might have the opportunity of telling his countrymen who had never heard it the glad news. He always refused to accept any payment for the time lost from his business. At last he was attacked by consumption, and to the end he tried to support himself and his family by making fancy articles of leather work. If any one among the Chinese Christians was in trouble or had sorrow of any kind, he would come to Hu in his sick-room for help and comfort. Though he had no money, his sympathy was always so ready and his counsel so wise, and the way he had of carrying all trouble to his God in prayer, made every one the better for a talk with him. He passed away to his rest in great joy and peace, leaving the memory of his bright example as a precious legacy to the little Church in Wuchang.

But I wish to tell you about the son of this good father, and how I was first led to take a special interest in him. One summer Sunday afternoon, when I had been in Wuchang for about a year, the afternoon service being over, I was sitting waiting till Mr. Bryson should have finished answering the questions of some of the congregation who wished to speak to him. My little friend, Chih Shwin, came into the room and began to talk to me. Now, it happened that I had in my pocket a small tract or leaflet, which had been written by one of the Chinese Christians. It was in simple ballad form, like many of the songs which the Chinese like to hear. Instead, however, of some foolish tale of the strange doings of the gods, or some sentimental love story, it told of a Babe which had a manger for a cradle, but at whose birth heavenly strangers sang sweet songs of peace and joy to all men. It went through the whole of the wonderful history in graphic, simple rhymes. The characters in which the verses were written were easy to read, and I asked my little friend to go over them with me. He tried to do so, but stumbled over many words, and looked so much confused, that a coolie who was peering curiously in at the door laughed aloud. "You pretend to read!" he exclaimed. "Why, boy, you hardly know a word!" Poor Chih Shwin looked quite abashed—for Chinese boys are as vexed at being laughed at as English children.

" How I wish I could learn to read better," exclaimed the lad. " Some time ago I used to come regularly to the school Mr. Bryson carried on here. Then he went back to England, and it was closed. There is no Christian school I can go to now, and father says I shall not go to the other schools where the boys must worship Confucius and the god of literature. How I wish we had a Christian school opened here again."

I wished that too, nearly as much as Chih Shwin, but there was just one obstacle in the way. You cannot open a school either in England or China without having some money to pay the teacher, and buy stools, desks, books, writing materials, and other necessary things ; and where was the money to come from? We thought about the matter a good deal, and prayed about it too ; at last, one day, when the English mail came in, it brought me a letter from a Sunday school in a town far off in England. It said that the children of the church of which John Bunyan once was pastor had sent me some money which they had collected, and wished to be used in teaching Chinese children. How glad the boys and girls were when I told them, and particularly some of the older Christians, who knew something of Bunyan and his wonderful pilgrim ! The " Pilgrim's Progress" has been translated into Chinese, and Christian appears in the dress of a Chinaman in the illustrations, with pig-tail and flowing robes. With this contribution we commenced our school, and though often we had very little money to carry it on, the gifts of friends in England, and the contributions of gentlemen in the English settlement at Hankow, have enabled us to keep it open ever since.

Chih Shwin was, of course, one of our first scholars, and we were much pleased with the rapid progress he made in all his studies. You would have been amused to hear him as he "backed the book," and repeated page after page of his Catechism, or the Boy's Classic, and chapter after chapter of the Bible. He continued to attend school for some time, till at last his father's serious illness made it

ENTRANCE TO A YAMEN.

necessary for him to do something for his own support. A sympa-
thising friend, who had some influence in the yamen, or official
residence of the Futai or mandarin, obtained for him the situation
of page-boy there. So Chih Shwin left school, and was at once
thrown into the midst of a number of men who hated the religion of
Jesus, and were always inventing wicked tales about the Christians.
He carried with him in his little box his school Bible. Sometimes he
used to feel tempted to keep the sacred book hidden away, fearing lest
the other servants might see him reading it and take it away from
him. Then he remembered all he had learned at school, as well
as the wise counsels of his Christian father, and determined that,
although he was only a very young soldier, he would not be ashamed
of his colours. He prayed for help, and God gave him strength to be
faithful. In his own little room, when the day's work was over, Chih
Shwin might have been seen poring over his book, quite alone; and
for some time no one knew anything about it.

But the mandarin, his master, was accustomed sometimes to go
round the house at night, when all the rest of his household had
retired. One evening he suddenly opened Chih Shwin's door, and
there he saw the boy, by the dim light of the flickering lamp, bending
over his book intently reading one of the beautiful Scripture stories.

The boy was discovered at last, and he expected nothing less
than dismissal from the mandarin's service, when he discovered
that he was connected with the despised sect of the Christians. It
was with a fearful heart that Chih Shwin placed his Bible in the
official's hand, which was held out to receive it. The Futai turned
leisurely over the pages, reading a passage here and there. Apparently the verses which caught his eye were such as met with his
approval, for after a time he returned the volume to the lad with the
remark, " I have heard strange stories of that book, but do not notice
any evil teachings in it; you can keep it if you like." Chih Shwin felt
as if a great load had been lifted from his heart, as his master left his
room, and his faith was stronger than ever in the God who was able to
protect him in the mandarin's mansion, just as He had preserved the

little Israelitish girl long ago in the home of the Syrian general. Not long after this the Futai's mother died, and, according Chinese custom, he was obliged to retire from office, and return to his native city, there for about three years to mourn her loss.

The mandarin had become attached to his little Christian page, and asked Chih Shwin to accompany him to the far-away province of Kiang-Su. So the lad went, and remained with his master for about a year, till hearing of the serious illness of his father, he gave up his situation, and came the long journey up the great Yang-tse-kiang, that he might see him once more before he died.

After his return to Wuchang he was taken into the service of an American missionary, who allowed him to come regularly to his old class in the Sunday school. His master was much pleased with the lad's industry and attention to his duties. After Chih Shwin had been with him for some little time, he felt anxious that a boy so bright and intelligent, who was also a Christian, should have greater advantages in the way of education, so that in the future he might be able to teach and preach the Gospel to his own countrymen. So Chih Shwin, through his master's influence, was admitted into a training college in Shanghai, where many young men are being educated for the Christian ministry. He has been there for some years now, and in time to come, the God whom he served in the mandarin's yamen will strengthen and bless him when he stands up to proclaim the glad tidings of salvation through Jesus, to those who have never heard it before.

CHAPTER IV.

IT was autumn in the Yang-tse valley, that fairest season of all the year in the far land of China, welcomed as joyously as the spring in more temperate latitudes. Fanned by cool refreshing breezes, the parched plains seem to revive after the fierce heat of the long summer days. Brilliant, many-tinted flowers spring up luxuriantly in every tiny bamboo-fenced garden plot. Gorgeous cockscombs of stately height mingle with sturdy sunflowers, whose seeds are used so plentifully in Chinese confectionery. The pomegranate's scarlet blossoms shine out like stars among its glossy foliage, and the fragrant olive perfumes the air. Chrysanthemums of a size and variety of tint rarely attained in England delight the gardener's heart.

It was at this fairest season of all the year that, some time ago, in a market town some twenty miles away from the banks of the great river, a little girl was born. There was not much rejoicing when the news was announced, even though the baby was the first child of the family. Indeed, I think the parents thought that circumstance only made matters worse. To have no son was trial enough, but to have instead a useless, unwelcome girl made their position indeed pitiable. But the mother's heart rebelled against the thought of drowning the baby-girl in a bucket, which was quite customary with her neighbours when a child came which they did not want, and somehow she managed to persuade her husband to keep it. It was wonderful how fond she became of the little one. I believe it was soon almost as dear as if it had been a boy. Before long a name had to be selected for it, and as no one would think of spending much time upon choosing a girl's name, they called the baby

"Nine," because she was born on the ninth day of the ninth month. This may seem very strange to you, but in China it is quite customary to give children names in this way.

Some people think that we are influenced a good deal by the surroundings of our earlier days. Little Nine's were simple and plain enough, poverty-stricken perhaps you would have called them. But people do not trouble much about comfortable houses in China. Even the rich know nothing of what we call the comforts of home, and little Nine's parents were by no means wealthy. The floor of their cottage was literally a ground floor, for it was made of beaten earth ; they had only one or two windows in the whole house, for it was considered very unwise to have more openings than were absolutely necessary, lest evil spirits should be inclined to enter by them. Over each of the windows they had a little piece of red paper pasted, with the words "General Chang Tai-kung lives here." This notice was put out for the benefit of the spirits who are supposed to be frightened at the very name of this general, who was a famous warrior of past ages. The walls of the cottage were festooned with cobwebs, and were very grim and dusty-looking. It was out of the question, however, to have them frequently whitewashed, for white was the colour of mourning, and the first thing they might expect after such an operation would be a death in the family.

But though you would not have thought little Nine's home a very attractive one, I think you would all agree that the market town in which she lived was situated in a very lovely part of the country, and that out of doors everything looked bright and beautiful. The little town nestled at the foot of a lofty range of hills, some of which were crowned with dark coronals of fir trees. The highest of all was a lofty peak, with three temples placed at intervals on its slopes, called the first, second, and third Heavens, the last-mentioned being quite at the summit. These hills looked down upon a vale of smiling beauty—a fruitful land, brought into a high state of cultivation by the labour of the husbandman. Small squares of many-coloured crops show that the land is divided into minute portions, for there are few large farms in China. Here were the light green leaves of the cotton plant, adorned with its snow-white balls; the drooping ears of rice, and the broad leaves of the tobacco plant and sugar cane. There are the feathery plumes of the graceful millet, growing to a height of ten feet; and the beautiful maize, its seeds gleaming like closely-threaded pearls, surmounted with purple flossy tassels fine as silk. Trees were more abundant in this neighbourhood than in many parts of China : graceful bamboos make many a shady grove, stiff dwarf palms spring up on every hand, and tallow and camphor trees grow luxuriantly. The low hill-sides are clothed with a growth of pine and maple whose rich colours shine out gorgeously in the fair autumn sunshine.

These were the scenes among which little Nine lived, growing strong and flourishing in the fine healthy country air. In winter she wore tiny wadded garments; but in summer there was not much difficulty about her wardrobe, because so little clothing was needed in the long hot days. Sometimes her mother would place her in a sort of half barrel, with a stool inside it, leaving her there to play alone for hours together. At other times she would creep and tumble about the earthen floor till she looked a very brown baby indeed. So she passed on from babyhood to childhood, and was soon taught to help her mother in cooking the rice and vegetables for the family. She learned also to spin and weave the snow-white cotton which had been gathered from the fields. Her life was not by any means an unhappy one, and she knew nothing of sickness till she was about six years of age. Then her mother began to bind her feet, and she often felt worn out with the pain the tight bandages caused. At last the pain was succeeded by a dull numbness, and Nine was discovered to be the possessor of feet so small that they were the envy of all the girls of her acquaintance.

It was about this time that the people of the town in which Nine lived were greatly excited by the arrival in their midst of a strange "outside barbarian," as they called him. What an extraordinary looking being he was to be sure! His hair grew all over his head and was cut rather short, instead of being nicely shaved off the forehead and braided into a neat queue, hanging for a yard or more down his back. And as for his garments, it was certain that cloth was extremely dear in his country, or he would never have made such a ridiculous figure of himself by cutting his clothes almost close to his figure, instead of having loose graceful robes, which everybody knew were the proper garments for men to wear. He wore a large wide-brimmed hat, doubtless that was to hide his unshaven forehead; and his boots were actually made of black leather, soles and all, instead of being white like other people's. Altogether this new arrival was such a strange-looking character that it was no wonder the children ran after him in crowds, and even the grown-up people felt compelled to take a closer look at a being so queerly attired. The boys would shout out "Foreign evil spirit" and several other bad names after him; and the mothers would sometimes reprove them, boxing their ears for such rudeness. But privately you might have heard them informing their neighbours that really when people made such frights of themselves, and dressed in the extraordinary fashion of these outer barbarians, they could not expect children to be respectful.

The people had many opportunities of watching the stranger, for he rented a house in their midst, and settled down there. They were never tired of crowding round the dwelling and listening for any strange sounds that might come from it, watching most carefully the while every movement of the foreign teacher.

They had plenty of opportunities of doing this, since the missionary had turned the front room of his house into a preaching hall, and might be seen there every day talking about the new "Jesus religion" he had come to teach them. Many people were constantly there listening as he talked, for the strange stories told about him made them curious. Some said he had come to kidnap and carry off their children; others that he wanted to gain converts to the new faith in order that he might extract their eyes, and make them up into the wonderfully efficacious foreign medicines. Not a few were convinced that he had been sent by the ruler of his own land to win the people over, and prepare the way for the conquest of China, which he doubtless wished to possess, since he had conquered the great Western land near to them.

Others believed that because the missionary now and then took walks in the surrounding country, he was seeking for some vast treasure of priceless value hidden away beneath the soil of their hills and vales. " For," said they, "these foreigners are not like ourselves; their strange light eyes can pierce far down beneath the earth or water, and see the wondrous treasures which lie hidden there." It was true that the stranger was seeking for treasures of priceless worth, for you know the Bible says, "What is a man profited if he shall gain the whole world and lose his own soul? or what shall a man give in exchange for his soul?"

After a time, when he had been teaching and preaching patiently for many months, the people began to understand a little better his motives in coming to their country. As in days of old, some hearts were opened by the Lord, and became lowly followers and simple believers in the Lord Jesus Christ. A few there were, too, who, seeing the foreign pastor was charitable, and had a heart to feel for those who were in trouble, thought it might benefit them in some way to join the new religion. There were people like these living in St. Paul's time; there are persons not very unlike them to be found in England to-day.

Little Nine's father was, I fear, one of these people; for he used to listen most attentively to the preaching in the chapel, and professed to have become a Christian. After a time he was baptized, with his little daughter, and she received another name in addition to her previous one, and was henceforth known as Happy Nine. The mother did not seem to become much happier, notwithstanding the change that had come over the family; perhaps the reason was that there was little reality in it. She found it hard to endure the jeers and reproaches of her neighbours because her husband had forsaken his ancestors, as they called it; and one day, in a fit of gloom, she took a strong dose of opium, thus putting an end to her life and Happy Nine was left motherless.

As the weeks passed by, her father was much perplexed about his child's future. It was difficult for a girl so young to be kept at home with no one in charge of her, and he had no female relative to whom it was convenient to send her. One day the missionary suggested that the child might be sent to a boarding-school for girls which some ladies had established at a city not far distant. She was at this time about nine years of age, and her father, after some consideration, agreed to the proposition. Happy Nine was received into the school, and found there many girlish companions of various ages. She was instructed with them in all household duties, while, in addition, she learned to make her own clothing, to read and write, and keep accounts. She was a bright little lassie, quick and clever, with a wonderful memory, and often during the vacation at the New Year's season, or in the days of summer, on her return to her home she used to cheer the missionary's heart by singing to him the hymns she had learned at school. It seemed as if she had quite left behind her the old life of ignorance and superstition.

And yet, though bright and quick when learning in competition with others, she was not naturally an active girl. She loved to sit dreamily, with her hands clasped before her, careless of the ordinary routine of work or lessons, quite regardless of the flight of time. It seemed as if her natural character was one which would be moulded more or less by her surroundings and companions. With good influences all around her, she chose to be good. Would she, when trials came, be overcome—too weak to battle for the right?

When Happy Nine had reached her thirteenth year, one day a messenger came to the school, bringing news of the death of the boy to whom she was betrothed. She knew little but the name of the lad, and her teachers were somewhat surprised to see how deep was her sorrow, and how violently she wept for many hours. Very soon they discovered that her grief was not so much for the dead as for the additional news the messenger had brought. Her father had hastily betrothed her to another lad, the son of some people who kept an opium den. They were willing to pay a considerable sum of money for a bright girl like Happy Nine, and had consented also to take upon themselves the maintenance of her father. Notwithstanding the low estimation in which the owners of such resorts are held in China, the old man felt it difficult to reject the tempting bribe; but Happy Nine felt the degradation deeply, and foresaw the miserable life that lay before her if her father's plans were carried out. Not long after, when he came to see her, she begged him so earnestly to delay completing the betrothal, that, although the cards had already been exchanged and a feast given to celebrate the occasion, he promised that he would not, against her wish, conclude the bargain with that family, and she must cease to fret about it.

No one believed Happy Nine's father but the girl herself, for everyone knows the binding nature of betrothals in China. It was, however, afterwards discovered that there had, indeed, been a rupture between the two families, since the keepers of the opium den, whose name was Lin, had refused to carry out their part of the contract, having declined to support the old man when they found how extravagant were his habits. Matters were in this unsettled condition for some time, and then, Happy Nine's father being anxious to arrange another betrothal for her, tried to settle the affair with the Lin family in an amicable manner. He offered to refund the expense of the betrothal feast if they would return the papers, seeing that they refused to carry out the contract in full. But, hoping by delaying the settlement of the business to obtain in the end a larger sum, they refused to come to any agreement with him. During this year of trouble Happy Nine appeared to grow more thoughtful than before, and one day asked permission to sit down with the other Christians at the table of their Lord.

She was old enough to be a teacher now, and her father, finding that his schemes for money-making in connection with his child's betrothal were by no means prospering, consented to her remaining in the school three years longer, on condition that the little money she earned should be given up to him. But the Lin family never relinquished the hope of finally obtaining possession of the girl.

One day an aged man came to the school, who looked as if he had travelled far in hot haste, and he told a sad story. Happy Nine's father was dying, he said, and longed to see his child before he passed away. She must get ready at once, and immediately accompany the messenger to her home. There was something suspicious about the man's behaviour, and Happy Nine, feeling afraid, declined to go with him. It was well she did, for it was soon discovered that the old man was in the pay of the Lin family, and had been instructed to decoy the girl away and carry her off to them.

Not long after this, Happy Nine's father was in reality taken ill, and died very suddenly. The Lin family felt that now their prize was secure, since it would be an easy matter to overcome a young girl's distaste for such a marriage. Old Mrs. Lin came herself to the school and painted a glowing picture of the life of ease and pleasure Happy Nine would lead when once she became her son's wife. She should have beautiful robes in abundance, and servants to wait upon her—and the elderly dame looked scornfully at the plain school-dress of blue cotton. But the young girl stood firm, and, because she knew there could be no peace or happiness in a home which was also an opium den, she decidedly refused the old lady's offer.

More than a year passed by, and Happy Nine's Christian friends were rejoicing in the hope that most of her troubles were past. It was true that secret messages had been sent by the Lin family, and letters conveyed to the girl in many ways, which it was difficult to detect, but she always confided in her teachers, and they were hopeful that the family's patience was wearing out. Yet once again old Mrs. Lin came to the school, accompanied by several of Happy Nine's early friends. She renewed her offer of a life of imaginary ease and pleasure. Was Happy Nine weary of the quiet routine of school life— not altogether unwilling for some entire change in her surroundings? I only know that in this last hour of strong temptation, when her friends were rejoicing in her victory, she suddenly consented to admit her knowledge of the betrothal, which was the point upon which they were concerned. Without loss of time she was hurried

M

away to a mandarin's office and made to repeat her admission there.

Then, taking off the simple school dress she wore, they dressed her in silks and satins and carried her off in a sedan chair.

Poor Happy Nine! Sorrowful Nine rather, for doubtless she has often since bitterly regretted that in the hour of temptation she so sadly yielded. A sad blight seems to have fallen on a life bright with promise. We can but pray God to keep her amid the evil that surrounds her; though in the midst of it, may she not be of it! Not long ago, on a quiet Sunday afternoon, a girlish face, weary and sad, was seen among the worshippers in the Christian chapel of the Chinese town of which I have spoken. It was Happy Nine, who, with a companion, had managed to come again to hear the blessed teaching to which she had once loved to listen in the happy school-days now passed for ever. Was she finding out for herself the blessed truth that "God is a refuge and strength, a very present help in trouble," even when we ourselves have helped to make the trouble? We pray that it may be so, and because we pray we hope.

CHAPTER V.

I CAN close my eyes, and see her face quite distinctly now. It was a gentle, lovable little face, with a bright, attractive smile. She used to wear her thick dark hair braided into a long heavy plait, which hung down her back. It was usually adorned with some bright-coloured fragrant flower, while, according to Chinese custom, her skin was plentifully dusted with white powder, and a slight touch of crimson dye was often seen upon her lips. She was the only daughter of the family to which she belonged. They were in very comfortable circumstances, and I think Chwin-E was dearer to them than many Chinese girls are to their parents. Her father was a Christian, and very anxious about his little girl's training, so he allowed her to come for some time to our school. She was rather a delicate child and her place in the class was often vacant.

"Where is Chwin-E?" I used to enquire of the teacher, when, upon entering the school-room, I missed her pleasant smile and the little hand that was always slipped so trustfully into mine.

"Ping-lian," or "She is sick," was the answer I frequently received. Yet though her health was by no means robust, Chwin-E was in one respect more fortunate than the Chinese girls of her acquaintance. Her small feet had never been put out of shape with long cotton bandages, for her father considered the custom so foolish that he determined his little daughter should never have to submit to it. So she was able to trip along like any English girl ; and though the children of the neighbours would often make great fun of her, laughing and pointing at her unbound feet, which, they said, were most dreadful-looking for a girl, and just like a boy's, I think they were sometimes inclined to envy her, when they saw how easily she could move along.

Time passed by, and we began to hope that Chwin-E would grow stronger. She rarely won any of the little prizes of illustrated books or English pictures which were given to the children who repeated correctly their chapters and hymns, but she was attentive and painstaking, and never so happy as when she succeeded in winning the approval of her teacher. But a day came that was sad indeed for little Chwin-E, when her father was suddenly taken away by death. After the days of mourning were passed away, the neighbouring women used to call in and see our little scholar's mother, advising her as to what they considered her duty. They were all agreed that she had been most neglectful of her child's interest, and painted in vivid language the sad future which they believed awaited her.

"The very idea of allowing a girl to have feet of which any beggar might well be ashamed!"

"Why, they were enough to ruin any girl's prospects in life, she would be fit for nothing but a slave girl."

Such was the unanimous verdict of the gossips of the place.

Chwin-E's mother was, unfortunately, one of those people who cannot bear to sink in the estimation of their neighbours, notwithstanding that the course they are taking is the right one. It seemed very hard to her that she should be blamed for submitting to the will of her dead husband. "If only they had been bound when she was little," she used to say, "all would have been well; but now, I fear, she is too old, her feet have grown large, for she is twelve years of age, and the pain she would suffer would be so great that, being a delicate child, I fear it would make her ill."

"What nonsense," was the reply of her neighbours; "we will never believe foot-binding can injure any one's health. It is just an excuse made by careless women."

No wonder Chwin-E's mother, who was a weak-minded person, with little resolution, grew only more perplexed, and at last, feeling

CHINESE COURTYARD AND GARDEN.

she could no longer endure the criticism of her friends, she one day procured the long cotton bandages and set to work to deform her little daughter's feet, and reduce them to the much-desired smallness which Chinese fashion prescribes. The poor child suffered more than is usual, since the binding had been so long delayed. She was an uncomplaining little thing, and bore the pain patiently, though I heard afterwards that she was sometimes seen in a corner of the house crying quietly by herself. When upon going to the school I missed her bright little face, and inquired after her, I received the same answer as of old. She was ill and could not come.

The fierce heat of a more than usually oppressive Chinese summer was upon us; even the natives suffered severely, and malarial fever was terribly prevalent. Sickness obliged us for a time to leave the city; and on our return, when I asked after Chwin-E, a sad story was told me.

Constant pain seemed to have sapped the poor child's strength, and when she was stricken down with fever she was unable to rally from it. She grew weaker and weaker, till at last, one August evening, they saw the end was near.

" Send for the teacher to come and pray with me," said the child; and when that good Christian woman came and knelt by the little one's bedside, she found the room crowded not only with sorrowing friends but with curious neighbours. With earnest words she commended the little sufferer to Him who is the Friend and Saviour of children in every land. The poor weak-minded mother stood by the bedside weeping bitterly.

" Do not cry, mother," said little Chwin-E; " I am not afraid! I am going to be very happy; why should you weep ? "

The heathen neighbours, who had pressed into the room, looked at each other in amazement. " What did it mean that a child could talk like that ? "

" She is not afraid; she is glad to die! What strange people these Christians are ! "

When they returned to their homes that night all that could change of Chwin-E was left lying on the bed in the sleep of death, for the little spirit had gone home to Jesus, " to be happy," as she had said herself. We could but pray that some of those Chinese women who had wondered curiously over the death of our little scholar might be led to seek the blessing of salvation for themselves—that wondrous gift which takes away all fear of dying, since Jesus says, " I am the resurrection, and the life : he that believeth in Me, though he were dead, yet shall he live."

CHINESE CHESS PLAYERS.

CHAPTER VI.

YANG KIEN-TANG ; OR, THE BOY WHO BECAME A DOCTOR.

MORE than twenty years ago, two members of the London Mission, Mr. Griffith John and his colleague, Mr. Wilson, set out from the port of Shanghai on a journey of more than six hundred miles up the broad yellow waters of the Yang-tse-kiang. For several days they seemed to be voyaging across some great inland sea, almost out of sight of land. Before long, they came to the city of Nankin, once the capital of China, and famous for its grand porcelain pagoda, which was destroyed by the Tai-pings, or long-haired rebels, who had been for years ravaging the country. Still onward by many a ruined town and city, past the bold peaks of Lu-Shan, and the entrance to the Poyang Lake, till at last, after a journey of twelve days, they reached the cluster of three cities dignified by the Chinese with the title of the Heart of the Empire.

On one side of the river, here more than a mile in breadth, stood the mart of Hankow, the great trading port from which so much of the black tea is shipped direct for England. Though only five years before, it had been burned to the ground by the rebels, it had risen up from its ashes, and seemed once more the flourishing town of old. On the farther shore of the river rose the yamens and pagodas of the provincial capital of Wuchang, one of the great centres of Chinese learning, which contains within its ancient grey walls examination halls capable of containing over ten thousand students. The small city of Hanyang was close at hand ; and a grand field of labour the three cities seemed to the newly arrived missionaries, longing to tell the busy thousands which crowded their streets the glad news which brightens this life with the hope of a glad life beyond.

The missionaries decided to commence work at once; and before the close of the year they were settled with their families in two Chinese houses in the midst of the populous mart of Hankow. Books were distributed, and preaching carried on day by day, both on the streets and in the missionaries' houses. The Lord of the harvest blessed the labours of His servants, and about one year after their arrival they had the joy of baptizing twelve converts from heathenism who professed to be trusting in the Lord Jesus alone, for salvation. One of the twelve was a teacher of the name of Yang. He used to be seen Sunday after Sunday in regular attendance at the house of God; but for several years

HANKOW, FROM THE HANYANG HILL.

his wife was bitterly opposed to his new faith, and tried by every means in her power to prevent him from taking their little son to the Christian services. Not unfrequently, however, the father's will prevailed, and little Kien-tang, with his bright face, was seen sitting by his father's side listening attentively to the preacher's words. Probably he was all the more anxious to understand what the teacher was talking about because he knew there was a difference of opinion upon the subject between his father and mother; and he was puzzled to know if it was right to worship idols as his mother did, or if the unseen God to whom his father made his requests, filling the while his childish heart with awe, was really the Being that people ought to worship. What strange stories the neighbours told of the Jesus religion, and yet his father was kinder to him than ever before, and at any rate no dreadful things took place in the chapel, such as people talked about.

Time passed on, and at last young Yang's mother became a Christian also, and would often come out to the chapel on Sundays; and at the same time, when Kien-tang was a lad of about fourteen, he also was received into the Church by baptism. He was a bright, intelligent lad, with an attractive manner, which won for him many friends. He had made good progress in his Chinese studies, and his Christian training was by no means neglected by his parents.

Towards the end of the year 1866, it had been decided to commence medical work in connection with the mission at Hankow. A fine hospital and dispensary were erected, and the lame, the blind, and those who were stricken with various diseases which the medical skill of Chinese doctors could not heal, came in crowds to the foreign physician. Large numbers were relieved, and went on their way rejoicing. It was only natural that a clever boy like Yang should have been much interested in this wonderful work of healing, and the doctor in charge, pleased with the lad's evident ability, readily undertook to train him for the medical profession. For many years he continued to study under the care of the successive doctors who took charge of the Hankow hospital; by each and all he was found to be an apt pupil whom it was a pleasure to instruct. One taught him a little of the English language ; and he made such progress in his medical studies that, as he grew up to manhood, he might easily have been placed in charge of the hospital. His fame as a skilful young physician spread among his countrymen, and not a few who would have been unwilling to place themselves in the hands of a foreign doctor anxiously sought for his advice and aid.

When Dr. Mackenzie was called away from Hankow to commence the medical work which has been carried on at Tientsin with such marked success under the liberal patronage of China's greatest Viceroy, Li Hungchang, the young man, Yang Kientang, found in a large degree the responsibility of the Hankow work

THE VICEROY LI HUNG-CHANG.

resting upon him. His home life was happy. At the age of seventeen, he had married the niece of the teacher, Shen, a man of considerable literary talent, and the principal native assistant of the Hankow church. An attractive Christian girl was the betrothed of Kien-tang, with quiet, gentle manners. The young couple were married amid the rejoicings of friends, both Chinese and English. Christmas Day had been chosen as the wedding-day; but when the morning dawned, the winter winds had lashed the broad Yang-tse into such furious waves that there could be no communication between the cities, and as the pastors were then residing on the Wuchang shore, the marriage was necessarily postponed till the succeeding day. Some two years after, a little son was born to the young couple, who received the name of Heaven's Gift. His parents received him as indeed a gift from God; and he has now several brothers and sisters, all of whom are being brought up in the love and fear of their Heavenly Father.

As time passed on, his fellow-citizens were proud to recognise the skill and ability of the young doctor. Some of the chief officials of the province became interested in the matter, and began to ask themselves why they could not secure for a purely native hospital a man so singularly talented as Dr. Yang. Money was readily subscribed, a building purchased, and Yang invited to take charge of it. After considering the matter, the young Chinaman consented to accede to the wish of his countrymen, but on one condition only. He was a Christian, and must be allowed to show his colours. If the hospital might be conducted upon Christian principles, and daily preaching and teaching carried on there, then he would accept the position. Nothing had been farther from the plans of these Chinese officials than to connect their new medical venture with the religion of Jesus, and yet, sooner than lose the valued services of young Dr. Yang, they agreed even to this distasteful stipulation.

The new hospital was opened on the 27th of September, 1880, with a Christian dedicatory service; and Christian preaching and teaching has been carried on there daily ever since. It stands on one of the busy thoroughfares of that crowded city,—a Chinese building, supported by Chinese money, and facing the doorway, in gilt letters, plain for all passers-by to see, is inscribed the legend: "To God be all the glory."

Thank God for a life like Dr. Yang's, and for the influence of such a life, which extends farther than we are apt to realize! Yang is not only a skilful doctor, but a most eloquent speaker, and few who have heard him at the Church meetings speaking in most expressive language of the things which make for our peace, but have felt a wish rise in their hearts that English Christians could hear him speak with the same eloquence and fervour.

A younger brother of Dr. Yang is now, after many years of study, preaching the Gospel to his own countrymen. He was always a clever lad, like his brother, and when only a boy was famous for the fanciful style in which he would write or paint Chinese characters. The Chinese use their characters or written words for many decorative purposes ; several words are written upon a silk or satin scroll and hung up in pairs upon the walls of their dwellings. Many clever Chinamen can take a word or character and make every stroke in it have some curious meaning, and looking like some particular object in the writer's mind at the time. This was a favourite amusement of the younger Yang ; and one day, some years

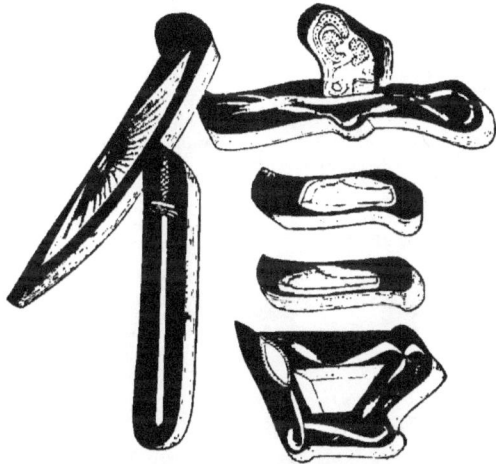

THE CHINESE WORD FOR "FAITH."

ago, he brought me, when quite a lad, the word for faith, which is written as you see in the picture.

You will notice that young Yang had evidently been studying the sixth chapter of the Epistle to the Ephesians, and has made every stroke of the character meaning faith stand for some part of the armour of God, in which St. Paul says the Christian is to be clad. On the left hand you see the shield of Faith, and below it the sword of the Spirit. The helmet of Salvation rests above the girdle of Truth.   Beneath these you see a Chinese shoe, for the Christian's feet are to be shod with the preparation of the Gospel of peace, and below them you have a side view of the breast-plate of righteousness.

A gentleman in Scotland who saw this clever picture-word was so pleased with it that he had it painted in colours on a piece of glass, which was put into a neat frame and sent out to China.   The last time I was in Yang's house I saw hanging upon the wall, evidently preserved with much care, the picture which had travelled so far.

CHAPTER VII.

KAI-KWEI; OR, THE YOUNG SOLDIER.

"SUCH a pretty girl as she was, with the tiniest of 'golden lilies.' So clever too! Look at her embroidery ; why, she could earn quite large sums by her beautiful handiwork ; and to think of her waiting for that young soldier ! Why, he had been killed in the wars long ago, without the least doubt !" These were the opinions and remarks of all the friends and relatives of a young girl, whom I will call by the English name of "Water Lily," who lived some years ago in the ancient city of Wuchang. She had been betrothed when quite a child to a boy, who was the son of a Christian. While still only a lad, he had enlisted in the imperial army, and had been drafted off with many more to reinforce the regiments which had been for some years struggling to put down the rebellion in the far north-west of the empire. Very occasionally letters would be received from him, telling good news of his advancement, but there seemed little likelihood that he would be able soon to return to his friends and home.

The Chinese are rarely in much haste to conclude their campaigns, and this one in particular had been carried on in a most leisurely fashion, the soldiers even waiting to sow the fields and reap the produce as they advanced upon the foe.

More than a year, nay, almost two, had passed, and no news had come from the young soldier ; so the girl's friends came to the conclusion that her betrothed had certainly perished on the battle-field. Even the widowed mother gave up the hope of seeing her son again. The friends of Water Lily having decided that there would be no soldier bridegroom in the future for her, were very anxious to arrange some other marriage at once.

Chinese public opinion holds in high esteem the girl who, in the event of the death of her promised husband, refuses to be again betrothed ; should she even put an end to her life, she is thought worthy of the highest praise. This is their ideal of what a virtuous and devoted girl should do. But, as a matter of fact, though a family feels that a great honour has been conferred upon them when a young lady acts up to this high ideal, I think, on the whole, to people who do not place honour and fame above all else, it is considered a more comfortable arrangement to have the girl quietly transferred into another family.

But Water Lily, unlike the majority of Chinese girls, was possessed of some decision of character, and having considered the matter, had come to her own conclusion. She had no wish to be married and leave her childhood's home, and she did not find her life by any means so dull and sad that she had any idea of putting an end to it. She knew but very little of the lad to whom she had been betrothed, yet she felt that without reliable news of his death she could not consent to act as if it were a certainty.

These ideas of Water Lily were very annoying to her friends, who were naturally inclined to arrange another betrothal for a girl so bright and clever. Had she not been promised before, it would have been quite unnecessary to consult her in the matter ; but with the popular feeling about the binding nature of such engagements, it was a very difficult matter to act in opposition to the girl's wishes. All the female members of the family had discussed the matter till it was quite threadbare, and they had reached the point of despair, when at last, one spring morning, the young soldier who had been so long missing returned "covered with glory." In other words, he had won the right to wear a mandarin's button, and a gay peacock's feather in his best hat.

The family perplexities were changed into rejoicings, for it was decided that the marriage of the young couple should be celebrated at once. It was the bridegroom himself who related to us, with much pride and satisfaction, the story of his bride's constancy, which

CHINESE SOLDIERS.

N

the proverbial little bird had carried to his ears. The marriage took place with Christian ceremonies; for in the rough life of the camp and the battle-field the young soldier had remembered the training of his early days, and was determined to have no idolatrous ceremonies performed at his wedding. This decision greatly dismayed his wife's friends, who were fearful that all sorts of evil and disaster would follow, if gods and spirits were not entertained and propitiated on such an important occasion. We attended the wedding feast, and tasted as sparingly as politeness would permit, the extraordinary variety of dishes which grace the festive board in China.

For some time after, the young bridegroom used to appear very regularly in his place at church, attired in somewhat gorgeous clothing, but a most attentive worshipper. He came up to the Mission House at frequent intervals, and had many strange stories to tell of his wild camp life. He informed us that he was well known as a Christian by his comrades, and one night he was captured, with others, by the foe. These enemies were Mohammedans, and when they found that Kai-kwei was a worshipper of the one God, and did not bow down to idols, they were much surprised, and had many inquiries to make. "We also worship the one God; we have heard of the name of Jesus!" they exclaimed. "We will not look upon you as an enemy," and the preparations for his summary execution were immediately countermanded.

As time passed on, a child was born into the family; but how great was the disappointment of the parents, for it was only a girl. The young father was a Christian, and his wife was trying to understand his teachings, and follow in the way which he said was the road to heaven; but it takes a long time in some cases to change the feelings and ideas about the events of every-day life, which have descended through countless generations. The young wife wept bitterly over the arrival of the poor unwelcome little stranger.

Then Kai-kwei took out his Bible, and turning to the third chapter of the Epistle to the Galatians, he read how "there is neither bond nor free, there is neither *male nor female*: for ye are all one in Christ

Jesus," and with these and other words he tried to cheer and comfort his weeping wife.

As the baby-girl grew older, I liked to see the young father proudly carrying his little daughter along the green slopes of the city wall, carefully comparing notes with us as to her growth and that of our little son. I think he had quite forgotten his first feeling of disappointment, for he tended the small girl with genuine fatherly affection. Some time after, the little girl had a brother, who was welcomed and rejoiced over, as are all Chinese boys, by every member of the family.

But perfect happiness, as far as the affairs of this life are concerned, is not any more frequently found in China than in England. Young Kai-kwei and his wife had hitherto been living, with little thought for the future, upon the savings of his soldier life. He had given up his post in the army because he did not care again to leave his home for an indefinite time; but it soon became evident that it would be necessary for him to find some employment in order to supply the needs of his family. Many things were suggested to him, and at last he was recommended by some of his Chinese friends to try and gain a livelihood by taking a situation with some foreigner in the port of Hankow. He would be well paid, and would still be near his home; these were very strong recommendations to Kai-kwei. So our young soldier was soon seen turning his hand to domestic work. I am afraid that the mysteries of an English kitchen puzzled him exceedingly. He soon found that his military training was the reverse of helpful to him, and before long he decided to give up an occupation for which he was by no means suited.

By-and-bye, a missionary who was engaged in itinerating work, and was in need of a Chinese helper and servant, engaged Kai-kwei to accompany him on his journeys. The wandering life suited the lad in many respects, though he would have been glad to remain at home, had that been possible. After a time he again accepted military service in the yamen of a mandarin. He was frequently on duty away from the city; but when at home, we rarely saw his face at the Sabbath services, and our hearts were often made sad to find the young man who had stood firm through the hard life of the camp, grow careless and indifferent amid the temptations of the city.

We hear very little also of the young wife, whose constancy and gentle ways had won her many friends. It is not right that a woman should be seen abroad, say the relatives with whom she resides, and she is kept very closely indoors.

Does she remember the old teaching and the good words she used to hear in the chapel? We cannot tell. We often have to work in the dark in China, to sow seed with little opportunity of seeing it spring up and bear fruit. Sometimes missionaries grow very weary and unhappy, because they see so much less of the results of their work than they expect and long for.

Then little hearts at home should often remember them, for even children can send much strength and gladness to far-off China by asking God to give it to those for whom they pray. When we are sowing the good seed of the Gospel, and it seems long in springing up and bringing forth fruit, there are some lines that now and then come into my mind, as well as very many beautiful Scripture promises.

Shall I write out the lines for you?

> " 'Tis weary watching day by day,
>   But still the tide heaves onward ;
> We climb like corals grave by grave,
>   But pave a path that's sunward.
> We're beaten back in many a fray,
>   But newer strength we'll borrow,
> And where the vanguard camps to-day,
>   The rear shall rest to-morrow.

It is God's work we are doing in China, and He has said that some day "the knowledge of the Lord shall cover the earth, as the waters cover the sea," and that "kings shall bow down before Him, all nations shall call Him blessed ; " so no one need ever feel discouraged. Do you think so?

CHAPTER VIII.

IT is well known that the literary men of China are much opposed to the Christian religion. At first, when missionaries went to their country, these scholarly men used to try and encourage the lowest of the people to rise against them, and when a mob was formed they would drive the foreign preachers out of the place. Very often missionaries have been stoned, their clothing torn from them, the houses in which they have been living have been burned or pulled down, and they have had to escape for their lives. Some have been obliged to swim across rivers, to escape away into the open country, or to take refuge in the yamens, or magistrates' offices, while the angry mob was battering at the door, calling out, " Beat or kill the foreign demons ! " Many Chinese Christians, too, have had to suffer the loss of all things because they have chosen to be followers of the Lord Jesus Christ ; some have even lost their lives because they would not deny Him.

The first of these Protestant martyrs in China was a man named Cheä, a member of the London Mission Church at Pok-lo, a town in the province of Kwang-tung. He had first heard something of the Gospel from a colporteur of the British and Foreign Bible Society, and wishing to learn more about it, he came up to Canton to receive instruction from Dr. Legge and Mr. Chalmers. He was an elderly man, and after he became a Christian he seemed to live only to bring others to the Saviour who had made him glad. His earnest labours were blessed by God, and in a year or two, at this remote out-station, which was only occasionally visited by the foreign missionaries, a little Church of more than one hundred members had been gathered together.

Such a good work could not go on without arousing the opposition of some of these literary men of whom I have spoken. They were very angry when they saw so many coming forward and professing themselves believers in One whom His disciples said was far greater than their revered sage, Confucius. So they determined to punish severely the venerable man who had been the first to become a Christian.

One October night, a band of cruel men came to Cheä's house and carried him away with them. They took him to one of their houses, and suspended him by his hands and feet from a beam. What torture he suffered all through that long night of pain ! but the Lord Jesus was close by his side, which made his sufferings easier to bear, for Christ never leaves His faithful servants alone in their time of trial. All through two days these men tortured and insulted the poor old Christian, trying to make him deny his Lord; but this Cheä had determined, God helping him, never to do. So on the third day they carried him off to the river-side, and as he still refused to renounce Christ, they put him to death and cast his body into the stream.

What a change it must have been for poor old Cheä to go straight from the angry mob shouting out for his blood, to the glad welcomes and rejoicings of our Father's House !

So you see the trials and difficulties of the Christians of early days, which you find described in the Acts of the Apostles, are being repeated over and over again in China now, which makes that portion of their Bible very frequently studied by Chinese Christians. You will remember that in those old days it was generally the wise and learned men who persecuted the Christians and hated them most, and it is the same in China to-day. No doubt, then, you will think that missionaries are very glad when they see these clever men coming into the chapels asking many questions about our faith, and then, after a time, professing to be followers of Jesus, and desiring to be baptized. Yes, they are glad ; but they are almost always afraid that these men are not really Christians, but are asking to belong to the Church, in the hope that some of the missionaries will be wanting teachers for themselves, or for their schools, and so be inclined to employ them.

There are so many literary men in China, because everyone thinks it so much better to be a scholar than to be a farmer or a merchant; and so a large number of these clever people are very poor, and always very anxious to get into situations. Not unfrequently some of these learned men will say they have determined to be Christians, when they do not understand what it means to have their hearts changed. They think they can become Christians by calling themselves by the name of Jesus; but we know that whether a man is an Englishman or a Chinaman he cannot become a Christian in that way. It is not only an outside change in our lives, but an inside change in our hearts that we need, and if we come to Jesus in simple faith He will work the change for us.

The missionaries have been often disappointed with clever people who have pretended to be Christians, and afterwards shown clearly by their conduct that they did not love Jesus at all. So they usually keep literary men waiting a long time before they receive them into the Church, lest they should afterwards bring disgrace upon the name of Christ.

I want to tell you about the two daughters of a teacher whose name was Wu. He was baptized in the summer of 1871, and in the next year his wife, with her two little daughters, Ta-ku and Er-ku, were received into the Church at Wuchang. Mrs. Wu was an earnest Christian woman, and she trained up her little daughters in the love and fear of God. But Mr. Wu, or Teacher Wu, as he was called, was a very different character. He could not understand what the other Christians meant when they talked about the happiness they had in following Christ. He thought, if he never worshipped idols, since he had given up the ancestral tablets, and came regularly to the Sabbath services, it was quite enough. He used to teach his little girls to read and write, consequently they were much better educated than most Chinese girls.

About three years after her baptism, Mrs. Wu's health, which had always been delicate, began seriously to fail. Before long she knew that she could not hope to recover, so she told her little girls she must soon leave them, and entreated them to remember all she had taught them, and try to follow Christ, taking all their sorrows and difficulties to Him in prayer.

Soon after, she fell asleep in Jesus. Not long after his wife's death, Mr. Wu began to think about betrothing his daughters, for indeed this matter had been delayed longer than is usual in China. He had no son, and therefore thought he would like to get a young man for a son-in-law who would be willing to come and live with him and act a son's part to him.

It is not uncommon for students who have obtained a high degree at the literary examinations, to advertise their willingness to become the sons-in-law of rich men. Mr. Wu discovered a young man whom he thought likely to make a suitable son-in-law in the person of a young military mandarin of inferior rank. When his little daughter heard of the negotiations which were going on, she wept bitterly, and begged her father not to conclude the betrothal, since the man was not a Christian. The girls had remembered the teachings of their mother, and as often as they were allowed would attend the Sunday services. One Sabbath morning the preacher took for his text the words, " Be ye not unequally yoked together with unbelievers," and dwelt upon the truth that the Christians who disobeyed this command, and married those who were still idolaters, could not expect God's blessing upon them. The young girl went home in great distress, and implored her father to allow her to remain at home unmarried, since she feared to disobey God's commandment. Mr. Wu refused to listen to his child's entreaties, for, he said, it was quite time she was married, and there was no one among the Christians who was not betrothed to whom he cared to give her.

So the matter was arranged. Before long the marriage took place, and the young wife came no more to the Christian services, since her husband did not consider it would be respectable for her to be seen out of doors. Only once or twice in the year, when she was allowed to visit her mother's grave, she would call at the Mission House on the way, and I was able to talk to her a little about her mother's God. But the home influences were too strong for her, and she seemed to have grown to a great extent indifferent to the subjects which had once so deeply interested her.

The younger sister, Er-ku, was still allowed to come to Christian worship at intervals, as well as to attend the women's Bible class held at the Mission House. I remember one afternoon the women had been holding a little prayer-meeting. When it was nearly over, Er-ku tremblingly lifted her voice in prayer : she asked that God would change the heart of her sister's husband so that he might become a Christian, and that the sister herself might not be led astray by her marriage with a heathen.

About this time Mr. Wu determined to enter into business as a cotton merchant, and he went into partnership with a man who lived in a town about a hundred miles from Wuchang. For a time everything went well with them, till Mr. Wu discovered that his partner expected him to pay all the debts, while he retained the profits. Mr. Wu was naturally very indignant ; but as an appeal to native justice would not bring any speedy redress, he bethought him that he might at least try what an appeal to the British Consul, through the missionary, would do for him. He was much annoyed when he found that, since he was by no means suffering on account of his Christianity, the pastor could not help him in this way. Seeing that this hope failed him, he declared his intention of applying to the Roman Catholic priests who would, he said, without doubt lend him their powerful aid.

Poor Mr. Wu! how little he understood the real nature of the religion of Christ. He was like many of the people who followed Jesus when He lived on the earth, seeking after the loaves and fishes, expecting that our Lord would be made an earthly king and give His followers power and influence in this world.

As time passed on, we began to be afraid that Mr. Wu would arrange a marriage for his younger daughter, and that we should miss Er-ku's bright attentive face among the little band of Christian women and girls. So we were much pleased to hear that there was some idea of betrothing the girl to Chang Swei, the young son of the preacher. I found that, contrary to the usual Chinese custom, the marriage had been proposed and was most desired by the friends of the girl, while the preacher was inclined to hesitate about the matter since he neither liked nor respected the father of Er-ku. The young people had played together as little children not long before, and consequently knew more of each other than is the case with most who are betrothed in China. Before long the affair was arranged at a feast prepared by the father of the lad.

Speaking about the marriage, the old preacher said to me, " Er-ku is a little older than our son—it would have been better had she been younger ; and the father is not all that we could wish, but we must leave the matter in God's hands. It has not been of our seeking, and certainly the girl herself is suitable in every respect."

So the young couple were married amid the congratulations and rejoicings of friends, at the little Wuchang chapel.

Their future seems likely to be a happy one, although, at present, according to a very common Chinese custom, the young wife remains in the home of her husband's parents while he continues in his situation as assistant at a mission hospital more than three hundred miles away, paying only occasional visits to his home. Er-ku's previous education has been very useful to her since her marriage, and she has often been able to give much assistance to her mother-in-law while she has had charge of the girl's school at Wuchang.

CHAPTER IX.

" SHE is very young," said the pastor, and he shook his head gravely. " Had you not better put off the wedding for a time ? "

He made this remark in reply to a request that he would that week go and marry a little girl about fourteen years of age.

Swei-ku was the niece of one of our deacons, and she was about the wildest Chinese lassie I ever knew. You would never have dreamed of speaking of her as having either a pleasing or attractive face. But she had a funny little twinkle in her small black eyes, and a comical expression of countenance which sometimes reminded me of Mrs. Stowe's " Topsy." I never heard what had become of her father and mother, for since I had known her she had lived with her uncle only. He had arranged a betrothal for her with a lad who was also under his guardianship, but it was not intended that the marriage should take place for some years to come.

In the meantime, Swei-ku was taught to earn a little money by doing needle-work, and to help her aunt in various household duties. She used to come sometimes with her relatives to the women's class, but her small black eyes would wander over the room, taking note of every foreign article it contained, and everything else was of more interest than the lesson. The rough little head with which she usually appeared made her a great contrast to all the rest of the women and girls, who always tried to look their best and neatest when attending the class.

But there was one soft place in Swei-ku's wild little heart, she was much attached to the little boy whom her uncle had adopted, because he had no children of his own. Whenever I appeared anywhere in the neighbourhood of the house, Swei-ku would make a rush indoors and bring out for my inspection the baby-boy, whom she evidently looked upon as quite a superior being to herself. But she was a very idle girl; she liked play very much better than work, and when reproved for her laziness would suddenly disappear for several days together, no one knew where, to the great alarm of her friends. Search would be made for her in all directions, but without success; and after some days Swei-ku's black mop would appear, looking in at the doorway, and she would settle down again as if nothing had happened, for some months to come.

These pranks of the girl's, which she seemed to regard so lightly, were very annoying to the family of her uncle. It was not at all respectable to have her playing such tricks as these, and after she had disappeared on several occasions, a family council was called to decide upon what had best be done with the refractory girl.

The advice of each one was that Swei-ku must be married—once make her into a wife and she would settle down quietly enough. Did ever any one hear of such a receipt for changing a mad-cap girl into a sensible one?

No wonder the pastor looked grave and shook his head, for the idea of wild little Swei-ku turned into a married woman was quite too extraordinary to be readily entertained. But as the girl's friends were all agreed that it was the only way to cure her of running away, and they had quite decided the marriage should take place, it seemed useless to refuse to perform the ceremony.

So on the wedding day Swei-ku appeared, her small rough head hidden from sight under the traditional veil of scarlet. As she stood by the side of her young bridegroom, a simple-looking country lad, I should not have been much surprised to see her make a dart out at the open door and disappear from our sight. But no such catastrophe occurred. Swei-ku made the proper responses and was safely married. She was marshalled out of the chapel by the two elderly married women who fulfil the duties of bridesmaids in China. She was taken to the women's apartment in her uncle's house, which had been decorated for the occasion, while the principal room was prepared for the wedding feast.

For some time after this I saw no more of Swei-ku; but when I next met her, I cannot say how it had happened, but a great change had come over her. Her hair was all drawn back in womanly style, and her forehead seemed strangely broad, for, according to Chinese custom, all the short hairs had been plucked out. She actually looked tidy for the first time. She was very demure and quiet, all traces of her mad-cap ways seemed to have been cast aside. " You did the right thing in marrying Swei-ku after all," I remarked to the pastor.

"Do you think so? Well, I hope so, too," he replied, though he still looked somewhat grave.

BOAT-TOWING IN CHINA.

CHAPTER X.

OUR preaching-room, or the "Glad Tidings Hall," stands on one
of the busiest streets of the city of Wuchang. It is open every
day of the week, and the missionary and native preacher are always
there for several hours at a time, speaking to the people, who curiously
peep into the room, and finally walk in and sit down, to try and find
out a little about the strange foreign people and the religion they
have come to China to teach.

Here you might see a countryman with the basket, full of things
he has come into the city to buy, set down by his side. Next to him
there is possibly a pedlar, who has left his case of cord and tapes just
inside the door; not far off are a company of coolies, who have been
waiting some time to be hired, or have finished some little business
of chair-carrying, and are now resting for a little time. Some of
them look sleepy and drowsy, and pay little attention to the speaker's
words ; others are puzzling themselves as to the real reason which
could have induced the foreigner to come to their land.

And now a group of young men, very imposing in their long
robes of coloured silk, have made their appearance, walking in a
stately manner up the hall, looking, in some cases, over the wide
tortoiseshell rim of their spectacles, they intimate that they have
some questions to propose to the foreign teacher.

"If this doctrine be really true," one of them asks, "how is it that
we in China have heard nothing of it for so many hundreds of years ?
Had it been really a religion worth believing, surely Jesus would have

been born in the great Middle Kingdom, instead of in that remote unknown little land of Judea."

They usually speak in this proud and scornful manner, for they cannot bear to hear of any greater teacher than Confucius, a Chinese sage who lived in past ages. He was a very great and wise man, whom the Chinese justly hold in the very highest esteem ; and the religion of the learned men of the land is called by his name. But he could tell them nothing about the future, for when some of the people who were his scholars asked him, he replied, " We do not know many things about this life, much less about the future. It is, therefore, quite useless to think about it."

One afternoon, several years ago, among all the various people of whom I have spoken, there came in a boy about fifteen years of age, whose name was Chang-Fu. Chang is as common a name in China as Smith is in England, and " Fu " means simply " Happy."

This boy sat still, listening to all the preachers had to say in reply to the many questions put to them by the congregation. At last the people began to go out into the street a few at a time, till everyone had gone except young Chang. The reason he had not left was because the preacher's son, who was a boy of about the same age, had invited him to come into the house for a little while and drink tea. This was the beginning of good days for Chang, for he became a very constant visitor at the preacher's house, since it was found that though so young he was quite alone in the city. His mother had been for many years a nurse in the service of a mandarin's family. This gentleman's family had removed from the city to spend some time at a house they had in another province, and so the nurse had left her boy in the care of a friend of hers, who consented to give him food and clothing.

Some months had passed since Chang's first visit to the Glad Tidings Hall, when his mother returned again to the city. She immediately set about obtaining a situation for him in the family of another official. The lad was to wait upon his mistress as a sort of page. Now this lady was, according to Chinese ideas, a most devout and pious woman; indeed, her friends felt that there was no doubt she had accumulated so much merit that the next time she was born into the world it would be as a man. For many days in the month, she would take no other food but plain rice and vegetables. Every morning she rose at dawn of day and burned incense before a little idol, which was placed in a beautiful shrine in her own private apartments. While she was performing these acts of devotion, it was Chang-Fu's duty to light the candles about the shrine, and assist his mistress in burning the incense. But while Chang-Fu had been paying such frequent visits to the preacher's house, he had learned that there was only one living and true God whom men should worship, and that doing reverence to these idols which men's hands had made was most displeasing to Him. The boy thought often of these things, and he became very unhappy; he knew he could not keep his situation without assisting the lady in her devotions. His mother would be very angry too, if he was disobedient to the lady, and yet what could he do, for he felt more afraid than all of disobeying the one true God?

So one day he ran away from his situation, and found his way to the chapel; and seeking out his young friend, Chiang Swei, he told him of all his troubles, and begged him to plead with his father to find some other occupation for him where he would not be obliged to assist in the worship of idols. The preacher, Pau, was placed in a very difficult position; the lad had made up his mind never to return to his situation, and he felt he must take pity upon him. So he employed him as a sort of errand boy, giving him his food in return for his services; and in this way Chang-Fu was received into a Christian home, and learned much more of that God, a knowledge of whom had made him fear to worship idols.

Meanwhile, the boy's mother, who had again left the city with her employers very soon after she had seen him settled in his situation, returned. In answer to her inquiries about her son, she was informed that for some time he had been an inmate of the Glad Tidings Hall. The neighbours, seeing the alarm and terror of the old woman, only

made matters worse by speculating upon the terrible things that might
have happened to the boy.

"He will certainly become a foreigner!" "He will eat the religion,
and those barbarians will be able to make him do just what they
please." These and many more were the predictions which only added
to the mother's anxiety.

In a very unhappy state of mind, Mrs. Chang made her way to the
preacher's house, and standing outside the door, she called upon him in
no measured words to bring out her son, whom, she said, he had kid-
napped, and she called the Christian religion and the foreign teachers
by all the bad names she could think of.

Then Mrs. Pau, the wife of the preacher, an earnest Chinese
Christian woman, came to the door and kindly and politely invited
Mrs. Chang to come inside and sit down, saying her son was just now
away on some errand, but as soon as he returned she could judge for
herself as to the way in which he had been treated. The poor anxious
woman was a good deal surprised at the kind treatment that she
received, but she waited with hardly concealed impatience for her boy's
return. Only those who know how a Chinese mother's every hope for
the future in the spirit-world is bound up in her only son can realise
how hard was the trial she had to bear.

After a while the lad returned. He told his mother all he had
learned about the one true God, and said he dare not worship or assist
others to worship idols. He told her of the kindness shown to
him by the Christians, and begged her to allow him to remain where he
was. The poor woman left the preacher's house that night feeling
very unhappy, though she had been somewhat reassured by the polite
and kind words of the preacher's wife. At last she came to the
conclusion that for the present she would allow her son to remain
where he was evidently well treated. Some months after, Chang-Fu,
at his earnest desire, was received into the Church by baptism, together
with his young friend, Chiang Swei, the preacher's son.

The members of the Church are accustomed to contribute a small
monthly sum for the relief of those connected with the Church who are

in extreme poverty or very sick, and for the expenses connected with their worship. Chang-Fu was only an errand boy at this time, but he was very anxious to contribute his mite also. In addition to his food, he received only six hundred cash a month, hardly half-a-crown in English money, but he asked to have his name put down for three hundred cash monthly. The deacons, however, would not consent to receive so much from him, as they thought it was more than he could afford to give, and he seemed quite disappointed at only being allowed to contribute a smaller sum.

As time passed on, Chang-Fu's worldly prospects improved, he obtained a good situation, and his wages were raised to about a guinea a month. Some time ago, when he heard that the Wuchang chapel was being repaired, he sent, as his contribution for that purpose, the sum of eight shillings.

I am glad to say that Chang-Fu is able to give his master satisfaction, and performs his duties well. I wish I could say that the lad's mother had become a Christian, but I cannot tell you this yet. One Sunday I was glad to hear that a new face I noticed among the women at the service in the chapel was that of Chang-Fu's mother. Since then she has been for a long time absent from the city, and I have heard no more of her.

CHAPTER XI.

PAU TING-CHANG is a man whose name is held in high esteem by the Christians of Wuchang. In former years he was a highly respectable merchant, and a devout worshipper of the gods of his ancestors. But he heard the Gospel of Jesus preached in the Hankow chapel; he became interested, visited the preaching hall again and again, till at last he determined to become a follower of Christ, and cast in his lot with the despised members of the " Jesus religion." In course of time he was elected by his fellow-members to the office of deacon, which he filled for some years.

In the year 1865, after much opposition, the consent of the mandarins was obtained to the entrance of the teachers into the city of Wuchang. These officials had done all they could to prevent the coming of the missionaries, for they argued that, if when the students came up from all parts of the province to the examinations, they found the foreign teachers living and preaching within the walls of the provincial capital, they would immediately consider they were countenanced and protected by the Government. This was a state of things they desired by all means to avoid. They had tried to drive the Roman Catholic priests from their midst some years before. Two of their number had been strangled by command of the viceroy, and their lonely graves among the rank grass on the low hill-side, without the city wall, were remembered and pointed out by a few who were in the secret. It was no wonder that mandarins and people consented only after long and wearisome delay, to allow the foreigners to enter their city.

The man chosen to fill the post of preacher in the new chapel which was built in this city was Pau Ting-Chang. His wife was a woman of character, and had been an earnest Buddhist, like himself. She was terribly alarmed and very indignant when she found her husband had become a Christian, and opposed him by all the means in her power. It troubled him very much to find that his wife became even more constant and determined in her worship of the idols than she had ever been before.

They had a child, to whom the mother was devotedly attached, a little boy a few years old. The little one fell sick, and became dangerously ill; the mother called in the aid of Buddhist priests who promised, upon receipt of a large sum of money, to perform religious services in the sick child's room, and save his life. They came and repeated prayers, beat their gongs, and burned incense; but all was of no avail, the little one died.

The poor mother's heart was almost broken; she lost all faith in her false gods, and, in her trouble, became anxious to find out what were the teachings of the Christian religion. You can imagine the joy of her husband when she told him she also had decided to become a follower of Jesus.

Another child was born to them, whose name was Chiang-Swei the boy about whom I am going to tell you. Mrs. Pau became as earnest a Christian as she was once a Buddhist. She used to train her little boy very carefully, teaching him to kneel by her side and repeat the prayers that little English children learn—the same prayers, though the words are in a different language. Her most earnest desire was that Chiang-Swei should grow up a good man, and a believer in Jesus. Her neighbours used to think she was far too severe and particular with him at times.

He grew up not very strong, but a bright little lad, dutiful to his parents, who were naturally very proud of him, and much beloved by all his friends. When I first went to China, he used to be very fond of coming up to the Mission House and helping me while I was studying the difficult Chinese language. He would tell me the news of the city, and explain many things I did not understand, stopping and repeating over very carefully any words which he saw were puzzling to me.

One day we made a bargain between us. Chiang-Swei was to give me all the help he could, as indeed he had already been doing, and I agreed to teach him English. How delighted he was at the prospect of adding a few more words to "Good-bye" and "How do you do?" which constituted his English vocabulary. I happened to possess an English primer, and so we commenced work at once. The meanings of the English words were all dictated by me, and written down in Chinese by my little friend, and then the sounds, as nearly as possible, were put down in Chinese, making a third column.

So anxious was Chiang-Swei to make good progress in the new language, that wet or fine, sick or well, he never failed to make his appearance at the Mission House. Now coming half drenched by the heavy spring rains, and now through the intense heat of the summer morning. The hour I had promised him was frequently extended, and his memory for long columns of strange words was most remarkable. A pupil so diligent could not fail to make good progress, and since every word he learned to read he was also taught to write, English penmanship had begun to be added to his other accomplishments.

As time passed on, the question of Chiang-Swei's future began to occupy his parents' thoughts. He expressed a strong wish to study foreign medicine, since the skill of the English doctor in healing diseases had impressed him and his parents, in common with most other Chinamen. Dr. Mackenzie, who was then in charge of the Hankow hospital, kindly undertook to train the lad. In the meantime, the Church of Scotland had commenced a mission in the city of Ichang, several hundreds of miles further up the river Yang-tse. They wished to open a dispensary and hospital, as a means of helping on the work, and were expecting a foreign doctor to arrive shortly. Mr. Cockburn, who is at the head of the mission, was pleased to secure the services of young Chiang-Swei, as an assistant for the doctor. So his training was continued by Dr. Mackenzie with that end in view ; and when the Ichang doctor passed through Hankow, on his way to his station the preacher's young son accompanied him.

Mrs. Pau felt it very hard to part with her only son, who was the child of many prayers, and yet she, with the father, rejoiced to see the lad going forth to take his place in the world. It was a noble service, too, that of relieving the sufferings of his fellow-countrymen, and at the same time telling them of a Saviour who heals, not only the diseases of the body, but cleanses and sanctifies the heart and life.

He went forth from us, followed and accompanied by many prayers. We were sending him out into a new world, far away from all his old associations and friends. He was only a lad, and had been carefully guarded all his life. Would he stand firm when surrounded by temptations ? Our anxious fears were almost dispelled by the earnest request which he made when he came to say good-bye : " Please do not forget to pray that I may be kept faithful to Christ."

Going forth in this spirit, not trusting in his own strength, it is no wonder that only good news has ever come to his Wuchang home from those under whose care he is working. Mr. and Mrs. Cock-burn have carefully watched over the lad, and have delighted to help him forward in his English studies. He has made such good progress that he can now read and write as well as speak English fairly well. Since the retirement of the foreign doctor, some years ago, Chiang-Swei, under the direction of the missionaries, has carried on the medical work alone.

He was married at Wuchang, some time ago, to Er-ku, the younger of the two daughters of the Teacher Wu. Rain and sleet were falling fast on the wedding-day, but within the chapel and the house of the bridegroom's parents all was bright and gay. The marriage was attended by a large number of Christian friends, the chapel was prettily decorated, and the many-coloured hues of the Chinese holiday attire made the plain building look very gay indeed. If the kind wishes and earnest prayers of many friends could make the future of the young couple a happy one, it would be indeed unclouded

Chiang-Swei continues at his post in the Ichang mission. A short time ago I received a letter from him, written in English. I think you would, perhaps, like to read it, so I will copy a part of it for you. Writing last July from Ichang, he says:—

"I am now keeping the Dispensary open with Mr. Cockburn, and there are many patients every day. There are more than six thousand since the beginning of the year. In Ichang, our Sunday school is doing very well. There are more than thirty scholars every Sunday. We teach them the New Testament and the Catechism, and make them repeat a verse from memory every Sunday. The war between France and China does not make any difference to us in Ichang, but our people seem to be very anxious to fight. I hope the peace between France and China will soon be settled.

"I constantly ask our Heavenly Father to bless you all, and help you to return soon to Wuchang to work for God. I hope He will keep you all in peace.

"I am,
"Yours very sincerely,
"PAU CHIANG-SWEI."

CHAPTER XII.

THE MANDARIN'S THREE DAUGHTERS.

In one of the principal streets of the city of Wuchang there stands a mandarin's residence, closely surrounded by the high walls which make the dwellings of Chinese gentlemen look more like prisons than homes to English eyes. If you were allowed to enter, you would see, as I have often seen, the prettily decorated courts, filled with gay stands of fragrant and beautiful flowers, the water-lily tanks, and the curious rock-work arches. Behind all the other rooms you would find the apartments of the ladies of the family.

In this home there were three young sisters, who lived under the care of several female relatives and a brother, their mother and father having died some years before.

They used to spend most of their time in working beautiful embroidery; the handsome decorations of their brother's richest robes were the work of their delicate fingers. Sometimes, when they grew weary of this constant work, they would play cards, or, what they liked better than anything else, listen to the gossip of the old women who came, they said, to sell flowers or powder, or some other trifling wares, but who were most welcome because they always had so much news of the outside world to tell. Just lately there had been a great deal of whispering and excitement among the elder women of the family when a certain old lady, who followed the trade of a marriage-maker, made her appearance.

Of course, they would have to go away from their home one of these days. How they wished they could all go together; but they knew that could not be. They had all been betrothed years ago, and yet none of them knew anything of the families to which they would belong in the future. It was certainly strange. The eldest of the three sisters was a girl of sixteen, the youngest only thirteen. One of the old women who came round was able to read. It was very interesting to hear her, and the girls often dreamed over the stories she read them. They were all about people the like of whom they had never seen; wonderfully clever young ladies, who could not only

A CHINESE COURTYARD.

read, but write most learned sonnets and rhymes; they met with the strangest of adventures, but nothing of the kind ever happened in their lives. They often wished that something new would occur to break up the monotony of their existence.

It came at last. One day, in answer to their puzzled inquiries, they found that arrangements for the marriage of the two elder sisters had been already made. How was it they had heard so little of the matter? they asked, in a chorus of voices. By slow degrees they discovered the truth. No wonder there would be few rejoicings when the wedding-day arrived, for circumstances had altered greatly since the day when their dead father had betrothed them as little children to the sons of two of his neighbours. The little boy who was to be the husband of the eldest girl had, soon after the betrothal, been taken seriously ill. People said that the marriage which had been arranged had in some way brought down evil influences upon him. At any rate, the lad had drooped and pined till he was now dwarfed and stunted and almost an idiot. But what about the second daughter? she, poor little girl, listened for the news of what her future was to be as if in a dream. When it came, it seemed to her that her lot was as hard as that of her elder sister's. The family of her young betrothed had become much reduced in worldly circumstances. All traces of comfort and prosperity had vanished from among them; she would have to live a life of degradation and poverty.

"And what of Mei-mei's future?" they asked; for even the dark cloud which had fallen over them had not broken the tender tie of affection which bound them to the little sister who crept lovingly up to them. "Oh, she will be happy enough; the family are rich and great, and their son is a clever youth."

In the quiet of their own chamber that night, the girls, who were little more than children, wept with each other over the hard lot that lay before them. What could they do? How could they escape from it all? Perhaps their brother might have some power, and could prevent the marriages from taking place; and if not, the elder girl whispered something to her younger sister which seemed to give her comfort, and they fell asleep. Very useless was the appeal they made to their brother on the next day; he was angry that they knew so much about their future. No one could break a betrothal—they well knew that. He was as sorry as the girls themselves; they must just endure it, for it was their fate. Poor children! they had wished so much for something to happen to break up the quiet monotony of their lives, and now it had indeed come. They would get over it soon, the elder women whispered. Of course, it was very sad news just at first, but soon it would seem easier to bear : no women were very happy in this world.

Night came at last after that weary day, and if you had looked into the apartment of the three young sisters you would have been surprised to see that they were all dressing themselves in their most beautiful robes, and putting on their finest ornaments. Could they be trying to see how they would look in their grand wedding attire? Their faces looked far too grave and sad for that. The little sister, too, seemed to be entreating them to allow her to do something which they at first refused. Then the little girl cried piteously, holding them fast with her slender arms clasped around them, as if she could never bear to part with them. "It cannot be any worse than this," the elder whispered, "and at least we shall all be together." Then she gave to each of her sisters something dark and small which she held in her hand. "No one knows anything about it, no one can tell us. I wish we could know; but no one does know." That was all, and then each of the children fell asleep.

When the first rays of a lovely eastern morning shone over the silent city, they stole in through the carved window frames, where the paper panes were cracked or torn, and fell upon three young faces which lay there as white and still as if they had been carved in marble. The sunshine lit up into brighter beauty the gorgeous hues of the rich robes of silk and satin in which the girls had robed themselves for death; but they could not wake the silent sleepers, who, knowing so little of either the joys or sorrows of this life, and nothing at all about the preparation needed for the next, had thrown their lives away.

Soon the shrill cries of the hired mourners were heard resounding through the house, mingled with the quieter weeping of those who felt what a blank was left in the household. Messengers were despatched, to see if the girls were past all medical aid, and some of them were sent to call in the help of the foreign missionary. They could do wonderful things, these strange people from the West; let them come and try their skill now.

What a sad sight it was for the missionary, to stand in that room of death, and think of what might have been and what was! How they might have been taught to look at life, with all its care and trouble, as means by which our Heavenly Father would lead them onward to the Home above!

But there are many more girls in Chinese homes leading lives with little of joy or brightness in them, and sometimes filled with overwhelming sorrow and despair. There is one thing only that can brighten these Chinese homes, one hope that can make lives weighed down with care worth living, and that is the love of Jesus. It is this message of glad tidings which we want you to help us to carry to sad Chinese homes.

CHAPTER XIII.

A CHINESE letter is lying before me as I take up my pen to write this last chapter about the young people of China. Such a strange letter you would think it, written on thin paper of a yellowish colour, with pink flowers and figures all over it. It was sent to me by a Chinese Christian, but it contains a message for all the boys and girls who read this book. It is a message of thankfulness, telling how glad the writer is that missionaries came to his country, and that he has heard of Jesus, and is now happy because he believes in Him. It is a message of earnest entreaty, because it tells how much more needs to be done before the many millions in that dark land of China can hear of that Saviour who died that they might live.

Before you read these words I shall be back in China. Shall I be able to cheer the Chinese Christians by telling them that many English children are thinking of them, praying for them, helping to send more good books and more missionaries to them? That would be a very good answer indeed to the letter of which I have told you.

When I was coming away from China, more than a year ago, a Chinese Christian said to me, "I may not be able to write you a letter and send it all the way to England, but every day I will send a message of prayer to Heaven for you."

That, I think, is the best kind of letter; and though you cannot answer the Chinese letter of which I have spoken, from the quiet of your English homes you can constantly send up earnest prayers for these Chinese children of whom I have told you, that they may be taught to love the Saviour, who put His hands on little children's heads and said, "Suffer little children to come unto Me, and forbid them not."

A lady was talking to me the other day about mission work in China, and she said, "I always pray for the Chinese people every day; and then I feel that I cannot stop at praying, I must do something to help forward the work among them."

Do any of the children who read this feel like that lady?

I know that some English girls and boys do. I have met with them since I have been in England. Some say, "I want to be a missionary when I am older," or "If I live to grow up I mean to come to China and teach the children about Jesus."

I have a little pile of letters also which I prize very much. They have each been sent to me with gifts to take to Chinese children. Many of these presents are pictures and illustrated magazines. Some of them are pretty scrap-books and albums, many of which I can see have been much prized by their young owners. But the little writers say, "We want to do something for Jesus and for the Chinese children." Another says, "I felt as if I must send you something for the Chinese children. Please accept these scrap-books and pictures; we hope they will give them much pleasure, and by interesting them help you in your work of bringing them to Jesus."

This is one way in which children may help us in teaching Chinese boys and girls. But there are many other ways, for money is needed very much to send out more missionaries. Sometimes men and women who would be very glad to go out to China and teach the children, cannot go because there is no money to send them; and yet there are still many large provinces, larger even than this England of ours, where they have no missionary at all, or else only one or two. Just think if there were only one minister in all England, how very few of you boys and girls would ever have an opportunity of hearing him preach. But that is how it is in China. Some people have never heard anything about Jesus before, and we have been asked, "Is Jesus the foreign Emperor? Have you ever seen Him?"

Just think for a moment about the terrible-looking idols of which

I have told you, that Chinese children are taught to worship at the age when little English boys and girls kneel down by their mother's side and repeat the beautiful words, " Our Father which art in heaven."

Then, when illness or misfortune comes into the family, they imagine it is caused by some evil spirit; and when at last the time comes for them to die, they know nothing of a bright life beyond in the Father's house of many mansions, but believe that a dreadful-looking figure, who is represented in some of the temples, comes with a heavy chain to drag them away to judgment.

But long, long ago, our ancestors in England were in very much the same condition, and were bowing down to idols and offering human sacrifices upon the mountain tops and in the forest glades. But Christian people in other lands sent to those who came before us the bright light of the Gospel, and so we ought to pass it on to others who are now in darkness.

What should we say to a man who had once been saved from starvation himself, and kept a large supply of corn in his barns, refusing to relieve the hunger of many who were in need around him? To the man who had been saved from drowning, who refused to hold the rope that was to rescue others? Perhaps you will say you are still very young, not able to give or to do very much. But have you forgotten that when our Lord Jesus was on earth, and wished to feed five thousand people, He did not ask any rich or great man to give out of his abundance, but took the five loaves and two small fishes out of the basket of a boy who was standing there ; and after He had blessed it, there was sufficient to relieve the wants of that great multitude?

The best offering any one can give, is to consecrate themselves for God's service in heathen lands; and it is not out of place that I should say this to boys and girls, for most of those men and women whose labours as missionaries God has richly blessed, tell us they wished to give themselves to this work, and decided, God helping them, they would do so, when they were very young indeed. One gentleman, who seems to have read a good deal upon the subject, says, in most cases he notices they were often not more than twelve years old when they first thought of it. And God expects every Christian to do something: to every one He says, "Go ye into all the world and preach the Gospel unto every creature." There are some countries in Europe where the law expects every man to be willing to go and fight his country's battles. The vacant places in the ranks are filled up by lot, and sometimes the lot falls upon a young man whose parents find it very difficult to part with him, and they will sacrifice almost anything, and pay large sums of money to induce a substitute to go to the wars in his stead.

Substitutes are not to be bought to go and fight their Lord's battles in far-off heathen lands ; but surely those who cannot go should make some sacrifices, should give up something they value much, in order that a substitute may be sent out in their stead.

God does not look so much at the amount we give, but He knows quite well what we are able to give. You remember when Jesus stood by the treasury in the temple at Jerusalem, He did not praise the men who cast in large sums out of their abundance ; but when the poor widow came by and cast in two mites which was all her living, then He commended her. But I cannot tell you what you must do or what you ought to give to help to send the Gospel to these Chinese children ; but if you go to Jesus and ask Him He will tell you; and if you obey Him He will make your lives very full of gladness.

And when at last the years of this life shall have passed away, you may meet in the bright land beyond the river of death with some Chinese children who through you have heard of Jesus' love, and gained an entrance there. Then how glad you will feel that you were able to do so much! how sorry that you did not try to do more to spread the knowledge of that dear Name which is above every name!

WILLIAM RIDER AND SON, PRINTERS LONDON.